Test of Fire

Test of Fire

GRAHAM GOOCH

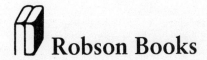

Robson Books

First published in Great Britain in 1990 by Robson Books Ltd,
Bolsover House, 5–6 Clipstone Street, London W1P 7EB

British Library Cataloguing in Publication Data
Gooch, Graham
    Test of fire.
    1. Cricket. English teams. Test matches.
    Biographies
    I. Title
    796.35865092

    ISBN 0 86051 663 6

Typeset by Selectmove, London
Printed in Great Britain by
Butler Tanner Ltd, Frome and London

Contents

Acknowledgements

I would like to express my grateful thanks to Steve Whiting, whose contribution has made this book possible, and to Stuart Surridge whose company of mastercraftsmen equipped me with the tools of my trade. You both in your own way helped to see me through this Test of Fire.

Introduction

For the most part this book was written as events unfolded in the West Indies and one drama followed hard on top of another. So it was good, when we arrived home in England, to look back, in something like tranquillity, at the successes and failures of our tour.

The first thing that becomes clear when I think over the tour, even though we eventually lost the Test series 2–1, is that, even if I had the chance, I wouldn't change a thing. Everything we worked towards was justified. We were a team of nobodies who were flying out to get a roasting in the West Indies. We had players lots of people had never heard of. But by the end of the tour we had made people stand up and realize that we had a team to be taken seriously once more. There was nothing to be ashamed of in the final outcome: England had re-established its credentials in Test cricket.

That was what I had always intended and worked towards: to be able to come back to England and look people in the eye again after some of the poor results we had been having in the past few seasons against all the major cricketing countries.

The players I took with me succeeded in doing just

that and I wouldn't have swapped one of them. It's easy to think that perhaps somebody else would have done better or provided more in certain situations; but those guys gave their all – and that's what people needed to see once more from England cricketers.

I certainly enjoyed being captain and I think the players were happy with me. I can't say I enjoyed losing – nobody does, but it's something you have to learn to accept in any sport. Besides, if it hadn't been for the rain that denied us victory in the Trinidad Test, I think we would have won the series. The West Indies would not have been able to play the way they did in Barbados and Antigua if they had been two down, and I'm sure the whole outcome would have been different.

It was the first three Tests we played (the second, at Georgetown, Guyana was completely wiped out by rain) that fully rehabilitated England at Test-match level. The first thing to say about them is that they were all cracking good games of cricket. And the reasons why they were so good was that England's cricket fully matched that of the West Indies not only in determination and commitment – which is what our training programmes had been designed to achieve – but also in technique and flair. Indeed, if one can criticize any of these three matches it would be the first Test. It was, frankly, one-sided: if it hadn't been for the rain, England would have won in three and a half days! The only time we did not match the West Indies – which was really our ambition all the way through – was in the last Test in Antigua where we were hit by injuries.

When we went out to the Caribbean in January, I wasn't really expecting to win the series. But at the same time, I wasn't thinking about losing – and certainly not losing as badly as we had done on the two previous tours in 1981 and 1986. One of my lines to the players was: 'Let them know they've been in a game of cricket.' I think they certainly did that.

I had to make it clear that I was the man in charge and I received all the backing I could have hoped for. All the guys gave me 100 per cent, and so did the management. They were right behind me, the players knitted together well as a unit, they listened to what I had to say and, by and large, they put into practice the things I had hoped they would.

It was a blow to me when I was injured in Trinidad and was ruled out of the rest of the tour. I don't like being out of action, I'm much happier when I'm fully involved. But I was never really downhearted, even though I had never been injured before. I had to accept the fact and I continued to grow into the job of leading a team on tour, enjoying it more and more as time went on.

I hope I can carry on leading England for some time yet. I hope to carry on playing cricket for several more years. I'll know when the time comes for me to call it a day – and even if I don't, I'm sure there will be a few around who will tell me!

My most lasting memory of the West Indies tour will be that we achieved the things we had set out to do. We did it by hard work, by application, and by a determination to put English cricket back on the right road. Manager Micky Stewart (who had been with England through the lean years) and I intend to carry on the good work as long as we are wanted. We are starting this summer against New Zealand and India, and I haven't forgotten that four years ago they not only beat us but that England failed to win a single Test against either of them.

1
Early Days

The trail that led eventually to my appointment as England captain in the West Indies was a long one. It had really begun a year and a half earlier at The Oval, when I skippered in a Test for the first time. That was against the West Indies, too, and it came at the end of a long and hard series which we lost 4–0 after drawing the first Test at Trent Bridge, Nottingham.

Looking back, I think what really gave me my chance was the spate of injuries – especially to some of our best bowlers – that dogged us throughout 1988 and on into 1989. We certainly went through some captains in 1988! Mike Gatting did the job at Trent Bridge, where we played our best cricket of the series. We had already beaten the West Indians 3–0 in the one-day internationals for the Texaco Trophy, and the draw at Nottingham ended a run of 10 successive Test defeats against them. I did well, scoring 73 in the first innings and 146 in the second, and we made a total of almost

550 runs for the loss of only 13 wickets. But they scored 448 for nine in their only innings and there simply wasn't enough time for a result. Unfortunately, Gatt found himself the centre of unwelcome attention after extra-curricular activities at Nottingham were splashed over the front pages of the tabloids.

Gatt was dropped and the captaincy for the next two Tests – at Lord's and Old Trafford – was given to his Middlesex clubmate, spinner John Emburey. But then a problem arose. The fourth Test was at Headingley, Leeds. In recent years England have often gone into the Headingley Test without a recognized slow bowler. Obviously it made no sense to pick John as captain if it wasn't even certain that he would be in the team.

I can say now that I was also in the selectors' minds at that point. I wasn't actually asked if I would be prepared to captain the side, but an informal sounding-out process was put into action after the Old Trafford Test early in July. Doug Insole, the chairman of Essex, who is a friend of mine and a man very close to everything that goes on at Lord's, started the process. I had to tell him that it might prove awkward. Giving me the captaincy now would mean that they also had me in mind to lead the side on the tour of India that winter – when I had already contracted to play for Western Province in South Africa. I explained all this to Doug, and the upshot was that the selectors brought in Chris Cowdrey, who at that time was not, of course, a member of the England team.

Chris is a popular player, but I'm not alone in feeling that he was not quite up to Test class as either a batsman or a bowler. There's no question, though, that he is a good captain – he had done a fine job leading Kent that season – so when he came in at Headingley I told him he had my full support. The trouble was, we now had a captain who had played only a few Tests and two key batsmen, Tim Curtis and Robin Smith, who were playing their first Test. We felt like a bunch of strangers – and this against the best team in the world!

Not surprisingly, they were much too good for us and we lost by 10 wickets. But Chris didn't do anything wrong, and I felt a bit sorry for him when he was dropped from the side after missing the fifth Test, at The Oval, with an injured foot. He was pretty upset himself and he said so – though we do not know what promises, if any, the selectors had made to him.

He had been made captain for The Oval Test but early that week he was injured when playing for Kent. On the Tuesday before the Test I was playing at Hampstead Cricket Club in a six-a-side benefit match for a friend of mine between some of the Middlesex and Essex players. Apparently Micky Stewart, the England manager, had been trying to catch up with me all day. Eventually I was called to the public pay-phone on the wall under the stairs at the Hampstead clubhouse. The phone is next to the bar, but over the din of noisy drinkers I could hear Micky say: 'Hang on, Graham, the chairman of selectors wants a word with you.' Obviously, they were at Lord's and Micky had Peter May with him. A few moments later Mr May came on the phone and said: 'Christopher is injured. We'd like you to take the team out at The Oval. Would you accept?'

So I said: 'Yes, with pleasure.' Naturally, I thought it was a one-match appointment, since Chris was injured. It didn't look as if it would affect my contract with Western Province. I had played there in 1982–83 and I had agreed to go there again in 1988–89 before England had asked about our availability for the tour to India. I would be able to take my wife Brenda and our children to South

Africa, but that would not be possible or practical if I went to India.

Then things began to change. We had Robert Bailey playing at The Oval, and he did pretty well in his first Test. Robin Smith made his first Test 50 and Neil Foster bowled brilliantly to take the first five wickets in the West Indies' first innings, when we dismissed them for 183. We left them to make 225 in the final innings, and though they got them with only two wickets down, it was England's best performance since the first Test at Nottingham.

I enjoyed leading England at The Oval, and in the subsequent one-off Test against Sri Lanka at Lord's. We were at the end of the season by then and I had had a good year. I had no fears about running a team on the field. I had played under some good captains, such as Mike Brearley, Keith Fletcher and Gatting, and I knew what was needed. I had also helped Keith Fletcher at Essex for some years where, although he was captain, we constantly exchanged thoughts and ideas. The fact that we had three other Essex players at The Oval – Neil Foster, Derek Pringle and John Childs – helped to make it easier for me.

Basically, I tried to captain the England side in much the same way as I had been brought up to do at Essex under Fletch. By and large, this means being positive in the sense of making things happen rather than merely reacting to events. My aims are the same in a Test, but you do it slightly differently. In a three-day game you can force things by declaring while you're still behind or by chasing quick runs. In a Test, things unfold more gradually. You play with greater caution for the most part because, over five days, there is a much greater chance of your errors being punished.

The ever-sprightly Jack Russell, playing in his first Test, brings up the rear as we go out to field against Sri Lanka at Lord's in 1988.

No need to run – I reckon I've got that one past cover in the Lord's Test against Sri Lanka.

Here I am in full flow for once during a difficult Ashes series against the 1989 Australians – this time I'm on my way to my highest score . . . 68 in the second innings at Headingley.

Dear old pals and jolly good company when I join up with two pals who have also skippered England – David Gower and John Emburey – during a practice for the fourth Test against Australia at Old Trafford in July 1989.

Green Cross code – the locals stand and stare as Nasser Hussain, Laurie Brown and Alec Stewart lead a training run round the streets of Trinidad. That's me at the back, by the way!

All part of the Manager's job. Micky Stewart seems to be enjoying a break in training to talk to a group of reporters and photographers – David Field, Adrian Murrell, Graham Otway, Chris Lander, Mike Beale, Brendan Monks and David Lloyd.

Some people say that as a captain I'm too inclined to attack. It's the way I was brought up. If it's a toss-up between keeping men in close-catching positions or placing them more defensively, I always go for the first option. I'm constantly looking for ways to change the field and to make things happen.

I want to put pressure on the batsmen by moving men in to 'bat-and-pad' positions or to silly mid-off. Generally, of course, you are looking for catches there. But sometimes you put fielders there not so much for the catch as to inhibit a batsman from playing forward, or to force him to make a rash shot which might end up in the hands of slip. The Australians used these tactics against me in the 1989 Test series.

Obviously, these moves don't always work, so then you try something else. You are trying all the time to lure the opposing batsmen into technical or psychological traps, based on what you know about their strengths and weaknesses. None of these things are learnt quickly.

There were other aspects about captaining England that I realized were also part and parcel of a job that had been carried out by some very eminent men over the years. I wanted to lead by example, not only in physical fitness and attitude, but also in appearance – something that is even more important on an overseas tour, where I feel one is representing the whole English way of regarding cricket. That also included setting an example in behaviour – little things, like being seen to have only a couple of drinks in the hotel bar each evening, and going to bed at a reasonable time.

Of course, after taking the captaincy at such short notice, I wasn't able to bring any of my own ideas on fitness and preparation into those last two Tests. As it turned out I didn't even complete the match at The

Oval. On the Monday I injured my hand when dropping
a catch in the slips off a no-ball from Phil DeFreitas and
ended up in hospital. Derek Pringle took over as captain
for the rest of the match. That was the second time I had
dislocated a finger when fielding to Daffy's bowling. The
first time had been in India in the World Cup. This time
my finger split open like a sausage when you put it in the
frying pan. 'Tiger' Surridge, the son of Stuart Surridge,
the old Surrey captain, drove me to St Thomas' Hospital
to have, as I thought, a couple of stitches before going
back to the ground.

But not so. At the hospital they were all very interested
in the cricket – the doctors, the nurses and everyone else
were either listening to it on the radio or watching it on
the telly. But a lady doctor looked at my finger and said
they would have to operate – and that I might be there
for about four hours. My wife Brenda and her aunt, who
were watching the cricket that day, came to the hospital
and took me home when it was all over.

Eventually I went back to The Oval, but I didn't take
any further part. It was the ring finger on my left hand
– not the most important one – and I might have been
able to play if I'd had to. But there wasn't much point
in risking it. Essex didn't have another game for a few
days, and I was OK to play in that.

Anyway, a fortnight after The Oval Test came the
Lord's match against Sri Lanka. I was retained as captain
and as such I had a say in the selection of the team. That
was the first and last time I had any close dealings with
Peter May, who resigned as chairman of selectors that
November. I never got to know him very well; nor,
I think, did most of the other players. We felt he was
a little remote, but I imagine it was his shyness that
prevented him from getting close to the team.

Anyway, we took on Sri Lanka at Lord's, where we were on a hiding to nothing. Sri Lanka were not a strong side and we were expected to win, so our victory by seven wickets was nothing special. From England's point of view the chief interest lay in the Test match debuts of four players – David ('Sid') Lawrence and Phil Newport – who bowled well and took seven wickets – Kim Barnett and Jack Russell. Both Lawrence and Newport were subsequently plagued by injury problems. In fact, their example added force to my determination to ensure that everyone selected for the West Indies tour was super-fit before departure from England. I'm not saying that Lawrence and Newport weren't fit and everyone has problems with injury at some time or other. But the fitter you are, the less strain the game puts on you and the longer you can stay in good condition. That's what our fitness programme was all about.

The old school of thinking was that you made yourself fit just by playing – by batting or bowling and by your work in the field. There's something in that. But it can't do any harm to prepare yourself up to a higher level of general fitness. I've never seen anyone in any sport become a worse player by being fitter and stronger than he was before. It's when you're not fit, and you start to puff and get tired, that your concentration goes and your reflexes let you down. Mike Selvey, the old Middlesex and England bowler who is now a cricket writer, pointed out to me that during the first Test in the 1990 series against the West Indies, at Kingston, Jamaica, both sides seemed to lose their sharpness when batting during the final session each day. That was understandable – the temperature was well up in the 90s inside Sabina Park – but a little extra fitness might have enabled us to maintain peak performance right up to close of play.

The fitter and stronger you are, the longer you can
maintain your technical ability. I've always believed in
that principle. I didn't have much chance to do anything
about it when I was made captain for the last two Tests
in England in 1988. But in the six months leading up to
the West Indies tour I had the chance to see some of my
theories put into practice, thanks to the encouragement
of Micky Stewart, who thinks along the same lines as I do
about these things.

We also had an inexperienced side going to the West
Indies and I wanted to spend as much time as possible
with them to get them thinking about their cricket and
understanding what I expected from them. It is amazing
that, even at Test level, a captain has to keep an eye on
his fielders to make sure they are aware of what he is
thinking and what he is trying to do. Very often you look
around the field and find that somebody is in the wrong
place, as if he is totally unaware of your strategy – even
of whether you are on the attack or on the defensive.
You may think that only Sunday-afternoon club captains
have such a problem. Believe me, it happens in Test
matches, too.

But I'm getting ahead of my story. I was reasonably
satisfied by my performance as captain in those last two
Tests of 1988. So it was clearly possible that, in spite of
my talk on the subject with Doug Insole, I might be asked
to skipper the side on the tour to India. Sure enough,
before the end of the Test at Lord's against Sri Lanka,
Peter May asked me if I was prepared to go to India as
captain. Naturally, I said 'Yes'. There was no indication
at that time that the Indian authorities would raise any
objection to the selection of any players in the party who
had links with South Africa. I had, admittedly, renewed
my links by agreeing to play for Western Province that

same winter. But players like John Emburey, who also had South African connections, had played in the World Cup in India and Pakistan a year earlier without any objection from India.

I don't think Lord's had done anything irresponsible or cocked a snook at the Indian authorities by selecting me and others who had played in South Africa. Ever since the Basil D'Oliveira affair in 1968, England have insisted on being allowed to pick whatever team they wanted, without political interference; the day they cease to do so will be a bad one for cricket. You pick your captain and your team on their merit as cricketers. No other criteria should be allowed to come into it.

I got in touch with Ken Funston, the old South African Test player, and Fritz Bing, president of the Western Province Cricket Union, to ask them to release me from the contract which I had signed during the summer. I owed them that much out of a sense of decency. They were good about it and agreed to allow the contract to lapse.

By then, however, the problems over the tour had already emerged. There was a lot of coming and going between our Foreign Office, Lord's and the Indian Government. It was suggested they called it off because I had been made captain. There were half a dozen of us with South African connections, but my name was at the top and the Indians were reported to have said that it was an affront to them to make me captain. To me that's rubbish. The previous year we had been accepted and granted visas to play in the World Cup. What had changed since then?

I didn't feel angry or even sad. I've learnt you just have to accept that politicians make decisions to suit themselves. In another year they happily accepted me to play there in the Nehru Cup as a result of the ICC agreement in February 1989. Yet I hadn't made any statements or promises about South Africa to suit the politicians.

I haven't changed my views over South Africa. I wasn't invited to go there with Mike Gatting's team this winter. As it turned out, I would not in any case have been able to go as I would be touring the West Indies again.

Anyway, that's all water under the bridge. Apart from 1988, when I had agreed to play for Western Province in the Currie Cup, I hadn't received an offer of a contract from the South Africans. I did have dinner one evening with Ali Bacher and Joe Pamensky from the South African Cricket Union when they were in London for the ICC meeting in February 1989. But they are both friends of mine and have been for a long time. I often meet up with them when I get the chance – but the question of my going back to South Africa on a rebel tour was never even mentioned.

Some people have wondered why I was prepared to take on the England captaincy in 1988 when, only the previous season, I had resigned as skipper of Essex. The answer is easy: there is really no similarity between the two jobs. I didn't give up the Essex job because I didn't like it but because it was affecting my form as a batsman, and I felt I needed to devote all my attention to that side of my game for a while. Last season I resumed the captaincy of Essex after Keith Fletcher had filled in for the 1988 season. By then the situation had changed.

The trouble in 1987, when I had to pack it in, was that I was expected to be captain, manager and opening batsman all in one. It couldn't be done. Not only did I have to look after the boys on the field, making sure they knew our tactics and game plans and all that;

I also had to make sure everyone was fit and ready before I could even think of myself. I never seemed to have enough time to prepare myself or plan the way I was going to bat. Often it seemed I hardly had time to put my pads on before I was out there to face the first ball. Last season we managed things slightly differently – I don't think I would have taken the job on again if that hadn't been the case. Fletch had become second-team captain, but he spent a lot of time with the first team, even though he wasn't officially designated manager. The effect was to take off my shoulders a lot of the little tasks I had been saddled with in 1987 – things like organizing practice-nets and the like – rather as Micky Stewart does with the England team.

I started 1989 with the prospect of skippering both England and Essex. But it didn't work out like that, as Peter May had already announced that he would not be continuing as chairman of the England selectors. I respected him, both for what I knew of him as a great batsman and for the work he had done for England over many years. He took a lot of flak from the media, but he always acted with the good of the game as his first priority.

The appointment of Ted Dexter as chairman, with Micky Stewart as his right-hand man, made little difference to my personal position. I felt that having one supremo, with Micky as his aide, was if anything a change for the better. The quality of the selectors is much more important than how many there are. But I still felt the Test & County Cricket Board had only gone half-way. They were rightly paying Ted to compensate him for having to give up his media work. But if they're going to pay big money I didn't understand why they had failed to go the whole hog and publicly advertise the post as a full-time, salaried job. Otherwise there was bound to be a feeling that the position was going to be offered only to a member of the cricket establishment, or someone with access to it.

Ted Dexter's first task, of course, was to appoint a captain to take on the Aussies in 1989, and the way that was undertaken was – from my point of view – disappointing to say the least. Three names were mentioned – David Gower, Mike Gatting and me. I believe Dexter interviewed David and Gatt, either in person or on the phone, but he never talked to me. Eventually it came out that Gatt had been the first choice; but that didn't become public knowledge until much later, when it was revealed that the TCCB had applied their power of veto. The only time anyone spoke to me was when Dexter rang me at home to tell me David was going to get the job.

That was fair enough. David has been a good friend of mine for something like 12 years and hopefully he will remain so. He is a great guy and a great player. But I was the bloke who had led England in the last two matches they played. David gave me a ring to commiserate. I just wished him good luck and told him I had played under him before with no problems and was looking forward to doing so again.

As it turned out, things did not go right for David in the series against the Australians. But Allan Border's side was absurdly undervalued before the Tests and turned out to be a well-balanced, fiercely competitive team. A captain is only as good as his team. Look at Clive Lloyd. He had one of the best teams of all time when he was captain of the West Indies. But with four fast bowlers as good as he had, almost anyone could have skippered them in the field. It's true he was a great motivator and he really got them going. But he was nowhere near as successful when he captained Lancashire.

It's funny how that old wheel of fortune turns. By the end of 1989 Ted Dexter had made me captain again. The irony of the appointment would have been relished by readers of the *Sunday Mirror*. On the Sunday of the Oval Test against the West Indies in 1988, Dexter wrote in that paper that my captaincy had the effect on him of a 'blow in the face with a wet haddock' – or words to that effect. He was entitled to his opinion and I don't hold grudges. But it is curious that he felt able to offer me the captaincy again only a year later. He has never said a word about that article and I don't suppose he ever will.

He's not the only one, though. There are some cricket reporters I find it very hard to get on with – not because of the sort of people they are or the way they behave but because of the things they write. But I'm never discourteous to them. They've got a job to do and they are entitled to write what they like and voice whatever opinions they like, even if I don't always agree with them and sometimes find them hurtful. What I find amazing is that they can write these things one day and expect me to have a friendly chat with them and give them quotes the day after. They really can't have it both ways. The thing I find most annoying is the way they lay down the law about tactics and captaincy and so on when many of them have never played the game at any sort of level. I'm not saying that if you haven't played at professional level you can't have sensible opinions about the game. You can, but you have to have played a bit. It's when they start to pontificate with that air of infallibility that I start to wonder what experience and knowledge they are basing it on. Moreover, they write one thing one day, and a couple of weeks later they contradict themselves.

The writers are lucky in that they don't have anyone to answer to. They pick out a certain player when a team is being chosen and often influence the selection by insisting that he should be given a chance. So the player is selected and, unfortunately, plays poorly. Immediately, the press get their knives into him, accusing him of incompetence or stupidity – mainly, of course, because he has let them, the reporters, down. As players we have to try to be consistent; I just wish some reporters would be the same.

Then there is another army of critics – the ex-players who are every bit as ready to give us stick as any of the press boys. Sometimes even more so. Some of them, great players in their day, really get stuck into us on radio, television or in the papers.

Sometimes you begin to wonder if you really have got it right when genuine experts like them wade into you in the tabloids. But eventually you realize that the papers hire these old maestros specifically to voice controversial opinions – and that their columns are in any case largely written by hacks at the newspaper offices. I've given up worrying about this sort of journalism. Cricket, after all, is a lot easier if you're perched in the press box than when you're standing 20 yards away from Malcolm Marshall or Patrick Patterson with only a bat in your hand.

In the event, the summer of 1989 gave the press a great deal to get their knives into as we lost the Ashes by a mile. As I have said, the Aussies were a very good team harnessed to careful and capable planning. We all wanted David Gower to do well and beat them. None of us wanted to play in a losing team and we started off OK in the one-day Texaco Trophy games in May. We won the series narrowly and there was a general feeling of quiet optimism among the boys.

We have a good record in one-day cricket – the best in the world over the past three years or so. It is a closer, better-balanced game and either side can win. In a longer game, such as a county championship match or a Test, the better team will most likely end up on top in the end, however much the game ebbs and flows in the meantime. Although some people at Essex might not agree with me, I am in favour of four-day championship cricket for that very reason.

David did well in the Texaco. He took the bull by the horns and opened the batting, making 36 at Old Trafford, 28 at Trent Bridge and 61 at Lord's. I was quite pleased with my form too, making 52 in the first match, 10 in the second and 136 in the last. I thought we had the nucleus of a good team with David, myself, Gatting, Embers, Neil Foster, Graham Dilley and others. But the writing was soon on the wall, for me at any rate. At Trent Bridge I was caught at mid-wicket off Terry Alderman, and at Lord's he bowled me (though only after I had made a hundred). That is how it went on, with Alderman rather putting the Indian sign on me. He always does well against me, whether in Tests or county matches. He bowls very straight, he moves it away a little, and umpires know exactly what he is trying to do. I was out lbw five times in the series – three times to Alderman, who also caught-and-bowled me at The Oval. It's true Terry wins more lbw's than most bowlers. Some people say this is because he bowls from very close to the stumps. I don't think that's the whole story: Neil Foster does that, but he doesn't get nearly so many decisions.

I tried to work out why Alderman was giving me so much trouble and spent a lot of time in the nets working on the problem. But it didn't seem to do much good and I began to lose a bit of confidence. That's why I asked to be left out of the fifth Test at Trent Bridge.

I rang David before the team was picked and told him I didn't think I was worth my place. My best score in the four Tests so far was the 68 I had made at Leeds, and I didn't think I should be in. I felt I was being picked on reputation and experience alone and it was time to give somebody else a chance. We had lost the Ashes by then, anyway.

I rang Micky Stewart, the manager, and told him the same thing. I don't think either of them was too keen on the idea of dropping me, but they accepted it. If they had really pushed me I might have been persuaded to play, but I felt it was in the best interests of the team. I wasn't trying to pick and choose my games, and I did agree to come back for the final Test at The Oval. But things weren't any better then! By then I just wasn't playing well – against Alderman or any of the other Aussies. Except for their tour in 1985 I have always struggled against them. Funnily enough, the West Indies have always been much more my cup of tea.

The 1989 Australians, well organized and well run by manager Bobby Simpson and skipper Allan Border, set out to put a big score on the board in every game they played. Look what they did at Leeds in the first Test: 601 for seven in their first innings! From then on we were always playing 'catch-up', for with that sort of total you can't lose and you have every chance of winning. It puts the pressure on the other side, who know their best hope is for a draw.

The Aussies' find of the series was opener Mark Taylor, who made 136 in that first innings and never looked back. I'd never even heard of him before he arrived in England; but Mark Waugh (brother of Steve) told us at Essex that Taylor had been the form player in the previous season down-under. He is a good player – steady, with sound technique and never flashy – and he played his own way. But he wasn't the only one. From being a team struggling to re-build only three or four years earlier, they had a side with class players like Dean Jones, David Boon and Waugh. Their fitness, dedication and team spirit paid off, and I knew there was much to be learnt from their success.

2

Ready for the Off!

On 7 September I was made captain for the winter trip to India for the Nehru Cup and for the tour of the West Indies. And the players for each of those trips were announced later that day. I had no idea they were going to pick the tour teams that afternoon, so I didn't have a lot of time to think about the players I might want. I would have liked time to phone some of the people whose opinions I trust. I did ring Fletch, but I might well have rung Gatt and John Emburey as well to ask them: 'What do you think of so-and-so?' or 'Which one is the better bet, this player or that?'

Some people seem to be under the impression that I marched into the meeting and said: 'I want him, and him, and him ... '. That's simply not true. All team selection has to be a consensus of several opinions. Nobody can have his own way on every player. It has been said that Wayne Larkins was my personal choice – that I insisted on having him as one of the openers.

But that's not how it was, either. What happened was that when the names for the opening batsmen came up I thought Wayne Larkins was the best player. He had a good season in 1989, which he obviously needed to have to be considered at all. He's always been a class player with lots of ability and in my view was easily the pick of the bunch. None of the others was picked for the West Indies tour on my say-so alone – except perhaps for my young clubmate Nasser Hussain. We didn't want too many young players on what we knew was going to be a tough tour; but I was confident Nasser would make a useful contribution as well as benefit from the experience. I had seen him play in tough conditions and I knew he had a good temperament as well as a lot of talent.

In the end, of course, the selectors have to make collective decisions. That's what our selectorial system is all about. I suppose the decisions that made the most stir in the press were the omission of David Gower and Ian Botham. 'Both' had in fact told me he was available for the West Indies and that he hoped to get back to bowling the way he used to before his back injury. His problem was that he didn't have any sort of season behind him to justify selection: he had averaged around 18 with the bat and 22 with the ball for Worcestershire, while his figures for England were only 15 batting and over 80 bowling. That sort of form doesn't justify selection even for as great a cricketer as he is.

'Both' didn't take his omission too well. He insisted that by the time the tour left in January he would have been back to his full form. But then a lot of players could have said that. What really got to Ian was that he was asked by Micky Stewart whether he would be available – and then was not selected. But he must have known that up to 30 players are asked every year whether they will be available to tour. That doesn't mean they will be selected – it just gives the selectors something to go on and stops them wasting their time picking a player who can't go.

That's the way the selectors look at it. But 'Both' chose to assume that, by asking him if he was available, they were as good as saying he was in. Anyway, what's done is done. I know that, being the sort of character he is, he will be determined to prove us wrong and force his way back into the side again.

It was a bit embarrassing for me with David because, suddenly, the boot was on the other foot. He had phoned me up at the beginning of the season to say he was sorry he had taken the captaincy away from me. And now here was I, as luck would have it, having to go to Leicester to play for Essex the day after David knew he had not been invited to tour with a party of which I had been made captain.

Ted Dexter was the one who had to tell him the bad news. I tried to ring David that night, but he was out; so I didn't have a chance to talk to him until we went out to toss at Leicester the next morning. He was very philosophical about it, as you would expect. He wasn't surprised to lose the captaincy; I think he anticipated that. On the other hand he had expected – justifiably, in my view – to be picked for the tour, and his omission did come as a shock to him.

So much for the tour-selection problems. On that day in September when the selectors invited me to captain the side in the Nehru Cup matches and in the West Indies, I had gone to Lord's to attend the county captains' meeting. I was looking forward to the meeting as I had a few choice words to say about the points deduction that had cost Essex the county championship.

We had been docked 25 points for a poor pitch at Southend. My view was that other counties had played on equally suspect tracks – most players know which ones they are – in many parts of the country. As a result of the Southend decision, the championship went to Worcestershire. They had a good side and they played well. But Allan Border told me that when the Australians played at Worcester in May and Phil Newport took 11 wickets against them, the ball was shooting and cutting all over the place.

In July at Southend the wicket was poor – there's no doubt about that – but, in my opinion, it was no worse than many others you see around the counties. Sure, we bowled Yorkshire out for 115 in the first innings. But in fact they had the best of the wicket – they just batted poorly. The top did start to go later in the match, but we managed to make 248 in our first innings. Yorkshire were entitled to complain when the ball started to fly occasionally later on – but I did not think it deserved the 25-point deduction. Moreover, both games we played at Southend in the season were of good quality and exciting for the spectators.

Earlier in the Southend week we had made 347 against Kent, so the pitch couldn't have been too bad then. I was keen to have my say at the captains' meeting. I felt that taking away points for unfit pitches was unfair, and half a dozen other county captains agreed with me. In my opinion it would be much fairer to impose a fine, which would penalize the club rather than the players. After all, the team only turns up at the ground at the start of play and performs on whatever wicket it is given.

As usual Essex were good to us. They paid the players the bonus they had promised for winning the championship, even though the loss of those 25 points dropped us to second place. Essex are quite well off and could afford to pay a fine. But many counties would find it hard, and that's why there is so much opposition to the fines system.

It was a bitter pill. But, all in all, we had a superb season at Essex, and I felt I had been right to take on the captaincy again. Our only failure was in the NatWest Trophy, where we went out to Somerset at Taunton. We were third in the Refuge Assurance League on Sundays and then, of course, there was that memorable Benson & Hedges final against Notts.

What a super game of cricket that was! Our only real error was that we didn't score quite enough runs. We made a respectable 243, but on a perfect day and such a good wicket, I would have liked just a few more. Still, we stuck to our task in the field and the last over arrived with Notts needing nine. John Lever bowled a superb over, with only five runs coming off the first five balls. He (like the rest of us) was shattered when Eddie Hemmings hit the last ball for four, but he mustn't blame himself. It was a good enough ball – JK pitched it well up – but Eddie moved inside it and got it on the meat of the bat.

Up to that moment I had felt the odds were slightly in our favour, and for three days afterwards I couldn't stop thinking about it and about how I might have prevented that winning boundary. No good, of course – if I'd had 20 fielders there would still have been plenty of gaps for

Eddie to find so long as he made good contact with the ball.

That was in July – and there were still three more Tests against Australia to come. I was made England captain on 7 September, Essex played their last game in the Refuge knockout cup on 17 September, and on 7 October we were on our way to Delhi for the Nehru Cup. A much-needed two weeks was the only break we had before we flew out to India.

As soon as we arrived we started training as a group in the normal way. But we made it clear to those who were going on to the West Indies and on the 'A' team tour to Zimbabwe that they would embark on a total fitness programme when they got back to England. Meanwhile, we emphasized the importance of developing the right attitude. We told the younger members of the team that, because they did not have as much experience as the established Test players, it was vital that they worked hard, were keen and enthusiastic, and made sure they were in peak physical condition. Then, whatever happened, they could return home, look at themselves in the mirror and know that they had done their utmost to give their side the best chance of winning.

Look at the West Indians. Everyone knows they have bags of talent. But what many outsiders don't know is that they have worked hard on physical training over the past few years, with their Australian trainer Dennis Waight putting them through the hoop, and that has helped them to become overwhelmingly the best side in the world for more than a decade. Until the end of last season they were showing us the way to go about things. I mean that up to that time they were far more *professional* than we were in terms of mental preparation and physical training.

Now look at our last two tours to the West Indies, in 1981 and 1986. You were picked, you had a physical examination three months before the tour, and then you were left to your own devices as to how you prepared before the flight out.

The 1981 tour for was quite typical. I had had a fairly good season in 1980, but I was left with nothing to do during October, November and December. Then I had a couple of nets a week at the indoor school at Chelmsford and did some training with West Ham United football team. But that was all off my own bat. If you didn't want to, you were not obliged to do anything. In fact, I'm sure some of our party just turned up on the day we departed having done no physical training whatever since the cricket season had ended four months earlier. That's hardly the sort of preparation you need to face the West Indies.

So this time, with the Nehru Cup starting the ball rolling, Micky Stewart and I were determined that things would be different. Nobody was going to point the finger at us in the West Indies and say we failed, if we were going to fail, because we hadn't prepared ourselves properly. And the Nehru Cup was a useful place to start, since all of our party apart from Nick Cook and Derek Pringle had also been chosen to go to the West Indies later in the winter.

Although we were finally beaten in the semi-finals, I think the Nehru Cup went pretty well for us – more or less the way we had planned. We played well in the three games that we won – against Sri Lanka, Australia and Pakistan – and Robin Smith, Wayne Larkins, Allan Lamb and myself all made runs. Then we lost three games, including the semi-final against Pakistan in Nagpur. But at no time were we outplayed;

and reaching the semi-finals was our original target, so we could not be too upset.

At Nagpur the game was restricted by rain to 30 overs a side, and we made 194 for seven, with Smith making 55 and me 35. It looked as if we had done it when the last 10 overs came up with Pakistan still needing something like 100 runs. But Salim Malik and Rameez Raja were in and they batted brilliantly. They are both good players and they were hitting the ball all round the wicket. You try to bowl to a plan when people are playing shots against you, but on that day we didn't get it right and in the end they won quite easily.

So on and off the field, apart from one near miss on the runway at Nagpur and a little bit of a flare-up, soon resolved, with the Australians, the trip to India went well. We got to know each other and I was able to make clear what I expected of the players in the way of fitness and dedication.

The business at Nagpur could have been nasty, though. We were taxi-ing down the runway after putting down a number of passengers and were preparing to continue our journey to Bhubaneswar when all of a sudden, out of nowhere, another Indian Airlines plane dashed up from our left and cut straight across our bows. Our pilot jammed on the anchors and, as we weren't travelling very quickly, we soon came to an abrupt halt. But there were some pretty grey faces all around and I called over to Angus Fraser, who had the best view from his window seat: 'Now you know what touring's all about, Gus.' The look I got back suggested that the big Middlesex seamer considered he had now graduated in that branch of learning.

The little incident with the Aussies involved their fast bowler Geoff Lawson, somebody I don't always see eye to eye with on the field. Off the pitch 'Henry' is OK, but he does get a bit excited when he's bowling, which is fair enough. This was our second match in the tournament, at Hyderabad, and Wayne Larkins and I were in the middle of an opening stand of 185 when I got a nick off Lawson that went to Ian Healy, the keeper. I certainly hit it, but I wasn't sure if it had carried to the keeper. I'm not saying they were deliberately trying to cheat me, but they had appealed. I stood my ground and waited for the umpire's decision. Lawson was getting really excited and he kept it up for a while after the umpire had turned down the appeal. Allan Border, their captain, came over and said: 'Are you calling our keeper a cheat?'

I just said: 'No. Like you guys, I'm just waiting for the umpire's decision. That's what he's there for. I'm not sure he caught it, so I'm waiting.'

The Aussies have a set policy of waiting for the umpire's decision. That's perfectly reasonable. If they are given out, they go. If not, they stay. But they can't have it both ways. If you do the same and it goes against them they ruck like mad – and that's double standards. After the game Border, who is a great pal of mine (and of course a recent clubmate at Essex) came over and apologized. 'We got a bit excited in the heat of the moment,' he said. And that was the end of it, though I don't condone that sort of behaviour on the field under any circumstances. The game needs umpires, and you should not, under any circumstances, question their decisions. If you do, the whole fabric of the game begins to fall apart. And cricket is too important for that.

After we returned from India towards the end of October, we set about the training programme that Micky Stewart had developed for the winter. Let's be clear about this. After our poor summer against the

Australians, Micky became the driving force behind
setting up a system to look after the players and to
provide them with regular get-togethers and training
sessions. We regard the West Indies system as the perfect
way of doing it. They don't have as many players as we
do. But they have a small nucleus of players who are
almost always with the squad, training and practising
with them, even though they may not actually be in the
team.

Micky's idea is to have organized practice and organized training for the squad, together with some of the
players on the fringe of selection, in the weeks leading up
to a tour. Sometimes, as with the 1990 West Indies tour,
there will be up to three months between the end of the
season and the start of a tour. Next year, however, when
we go to Australia, there may be no more than a month
or so. Then the programme will have to be tailored to
fit. I don't yet know exactly what Micky will want but
perhaps we'll have a week or so at Lilleshall, and the
rest of the time the lads will have to keep to their set
training programmes.

Micky really chased around setting up this programme. He established six centres – at Chelmsford,
Cheltenham, Lord's, Leeds, Northampton and East
Molesey in Surrey. Then he called in Colin Tomlin, who
was athletics coach at Kent University in Canterbury and
had helped Kent with their training, and John Brewer,
who is with the F.A. Human Performance Centre at
Lilleshall, where football clubs can take their players
to test their level of fitness. Finally Micky enlisted the
help of a number of former cricketers, who were all
keen to see English cricket back on its feet again.
David Lloyd and Geoff Boycott were assigned to Leeds,
Bob Carter to Northampton, Bob Cottam and Norman

Gifford went to Cheltenham, Graham Saville and I to Chelmsford, Lord's had Don Wilson, Geoff Arnold and Les Lenham, the last two also being assigned to East Molesey. Alan Knott, the wicket-keeping coach, shuttled between Cheltenham and East Molesey where he could keep an eye on Jack Russell and Alec Stewart. We set up a programme which consisted basically of running and circuit training several times a week, interspersed with net practice two or three times a week. By having several centres we could cut down on the travelling, which otherwise might have become almost impossible and certainly exhausting.

First of all, everybody had a medical examination on which his fitness assessment was based. Then everybody was given a 'circuit' – a series of exercises they had to do at least twice a week – and also a number of runs, from sprints up to a maximum of five miles. The programme was varied each week. Everyone in the tour parties had the same programme: but the ones who scored highest in the fitness assessments were required, for instance, to complete the sprints and longer runs in better times than the less fit players.

Micky Stewart was at the centre of it all, working and planning and running around. I can't say whether he saw in me a captain who was going to go along with his plans, but he knew I was keen on fitness and we had talked about it many times. So he knew that I was not going to argue with him about what he was doing.

Cricket is a very tough game, and many people don't realize what it can take out of you. You can arrive back at your hotel or home after a day's cricket, be it a one-day match or a five-day Test, feeling completely exhausted. Sometimes I just flake out on the bed. I'm always feeling drowsy by about nine o'clock and more often than not I'm asleep by ten or half past.

I'm sure that many England captains in the past decade would have gone along with our fitness programme. David Gower, for one, I'm certain would have backed it; so would Mike Gatting. And Micky has been the ideal man to run it. He has all the zip and enthusiasm from his days as a professional footballer with Charlton. He buzzes around, advising here, cajoling there. He will never be angry if somebody fails just because the other man is too good for them on the day – but woe betide anyone who doesn't give his all. He never bawls you out, but relies on a little joke and a quiet comment to let you know what he's thinking. He doesn't miss a thing, either. Not for him the occasional stroll round the ground to relax. He sits and watches every ball and at the end of the day he knows exactly how many half volleys we have bowled.

Micky is very conscientious too. I believe that when he was manager of Surrey he logged the result of every ball they bowled. He didn't quite do that with us, but he kept an eye on everything we did. At the end of a session in the field he would come up to me and tell me if he thought I had done something wrong and perhaps make one or two suggestions on different ways to go about things. But they were always only suggestions. Micky respected the fact that I was captain and he knew the final decisions lay with me. He would also take a note of any error he might see creeping into anyone's play and, since he was also our coach on tour, he would iron matters out at nets. Of course, as professionals, we should be pretty good players, with an understanding of the basic mechanics of technique; but faults can still creep in without our noticing them.

It was up to me and vice-captain Allan Lamb, in particular, to use our experience to give Micky a hand; and of course we received a lot of help during the winter from the coaches he had signed up. Each of them possessed expertise in one or more of the different skills of the game – batting, bowling and keeping wicket. It was striking that a batsman-coach such as Geoff Boycott would often be of as much help to bowlers as he was to batsmen, as he could tell them the sort of deliveries particular players would rather not face.

I think most people appreciated the efforts we were making to ensure that we were the fittest and best-prepared cricket team ever to leave these shores. But I was asked one extraordinary question at the press conference we held at Lilleshall when the training was almost complete. 'You've had all the training programme and you've done all the fitness stuff,' a reporter said. 'What's the position if things don't go well in the West Indies? Is all this training programme going out the window?'

This man obviously had no idea what the programme was all about. We felt it was right to prepare ourselves in every possible way to play professional international cricket to the best of our ability. That objective was, to anyone with a morsel of sense, the correct one whether we won or lost. Soccer clubs train all week to hone their skills and their fitness. If they go out on a Saturday afternoon and get beaten, it doesn't mean they don't bother to train the following week for the next game. If anything, they train all the harder and do their best to put things right.

We've started this thing now, and I hope it will be taken forwards as a regular part of our cricket curriculum. And I'd like to be involved with it when

I pack up playing. Cricket has been my life since I was a young lad, and I would like to put something back into it. I would like to start with Essex, who have been close to me all my life. I also have a job as a representative with Stuart Surridge, the bat-makers, whose Witham factory is only a few minutes from my home in Brentwood. This, too, will keep me involved with the game.

Don't write me off just yet, though. I hope to keep on playing county cricket for many more years, though I can't see myself playing international cricket a lot longer. I know people like Viv Richards, Gordon Greenidge, Sunil Gavaskar and others have continued their Test careers into their late 30s or beyond, but you can't rely on being able to do that. Even now I don't think I'm playing quite as well as I used to, but that doesn't mean I can't perform well. One's reflexes and reactions lose a little of their sharpness, but you can make up for that with your extra experience. You just have to be realistic. Somebody like Wayne Larkins, who is 36 now, knows he can't go on for ever, but he has had a chance to pick up a Test career that a few seasons ago looked as if it might be over almost before it had started, and now he can have one or two good years. The main thing is to realize when it's time to pack it in so you can quit while you're at or near the top. I'm sure I will know when that time comes.

Anyway, by the fourth week in January we had completed our fitness training programme in England and were preparing to fly to the West Indies. We were raring to go.

3

Down to Work

On Tuesday, 23 January we were on our way. The team gathered at the Copthorne Hotel, on the outskirts of Gatwick Airport in Sussex, the night before. I said goodbye to my wife Brenda and our three daughters and then it was off round the M25 in time for a team get-together at the hotel. In the morning it was all aboard the British Airways jumbo and away to our first stop, Barbados. What lay ahead during the next three months, only time would tell. At least we were confident that no English team had ever been better prepared. That was all I could ask.

We were met at the Grantley Adams International Airport by the usual official welcoming committee – and by a West Indian cricket press anxious for a first look at these untried and unsung English cricketers who had the temerity to challenge their world champions. In the event their questions were few and routine. Perhaps they had already made up their minds on what the mighty West

Indies were going to do to us. For them the coming Test series was a one-horse race, and we weren't that horse. I didn't mind that. The more the pundits wrote us off, the better I liked it. I could use it to our advantage when I spoke to our lads – use it as a weapon to stir them up and make them determined to prove the experts wrong.

I took the opportunity to speak to Tony Cozier, the well-known cricket commentator and writer, who lives in Barbados. Tony, a white Barbadian, whose father covered the famous Ramadhin and Valentine Test match at Lord's in 1950, is the recognized authority on West Indian cricket. And what he told me served only to make me more determined than ever.

He reckoned that most people had written us off already, but that we could still generate interest in the tour if we did well in the first two one-day internationals, due to be played in Trinidad at the end of the first three weeks.

Tony thought that if we were slaughtered in the one-day games, the Caribbean public would dismiss the Test series as a non-event. I was as keen as anyone could be to make this tour a success. But once I had heard at first hand what the local attitude was, I was determined to make the lads keener than ever. We would never go on the field and just go through the motions. We would never go out there thinking: 'We'll try our best and if it goes well, all well and good. But if it doesn't, then there's another day tomorrow.' That could never be the attitude of any team led by me, be it a Test team, a county team – or some side on the village green.

You have to go out believing you are going to win. I'm a firm believer that winning is a habit. But so is losing. It's up to us which habit we acquire. If you get into the winning habit, you *expect* to win; then, if you get into a position where things are a bit tight, you can still pull through by drawing on your experience of winning. On the other hand, sides sometimes play well for most of a game, but then throw everything away because they lose their nerve. If you like, they're almost afraid of winning.

One of the high-spots of our arrival at Grantley Adams was the number of members of the Ellcock family who were there to greet Ricky. The Middlesex bowler was born in Barbados and had played for the island before moving to England. Naturally the local photographers wanted pictures of him and our other West Indian-born players. It was very sad when Ricky had to go home from St Lucia after only a fortnight with a recurrence of his back injury.

He had been picked on merit as an exciting, very pacy fast bowler. The selectors knew he had a history of back trouble, so his selection was a bit of a gamble. But at the end of the season he had been fit. Unfortunately his back problem flared up again, and although we gave him time to see if it cleared up, it eventually became obvious that it was best for him – as well as for Middlesex and England – to return home for treatment. Our feelings at the time were that if he had to have an operation, and possibly even miss a season, he was still young, and it would be the best thing for him in the long run.

It was a sad decision to have to make and young Ricky was really upset. But he had a final try-out in the nets at St Lucia, and when his back stiffened up again afterwards, there was no alternative. After talking to Keith Fletcher, who was in Nairobi managing the England 'A' tour to Zimbabwe and Kenya, we decided to call in Leicestershire's young Chris Lewis, who didn't reduce our West Indian contingent since he was born in Guyana.

We had a week in Barbados, practising and getting used to the sun. We were staying at Rockley Resort Hotel, which is not on the beach but conveniently placed in the middle of a golf course.

There wasn't much sun on the first day, though: nets were washed out by rain. And on the second day we had our first setback when Allan Lamb was injured. Lambie, Robin Smith and I had decided to jog back to the hotel after finishing our net practice and training at Kensington Oval in Bridgetown were over. It was a gentle run of about four miles and there shouldn't have been any problems. But Lambie stepped awkwardly up a kerb and damaged a calf muscle. Micky Stewart was not over-impressed and told us so in a few short, crisp phrases. But I don't feel we did anything too silly. Maybe we shouldn't have run back after such a tough work-out; but we were warm and toned up. It was just one of those things that can always happen.

The two practice matches in Barbados, after we'd been there almost a week, went well enough and gave us a good work-out in the middle. But we only just beat a young Barbados side, who gave us a bit of a fright. In a way it was a good thing, and it was all the help I needed to hammer home the message that there would be no easy matches in the West Indies and we would have to be on the ball the whole time. We set them 238 to win and they got off to a flyer. Then they lost half a dozen wickets quickly, and we were cruising home until their number 10 started to smash the ball about. We finally dismissed them with a couple of overs to spare. But we hadn't been very convincing, and it was useful for us to

Devon Malcolm winds up to let one go during the first Test in
Jamaica where his match haul of five for 126 played a big part in our
nine wickets victory.

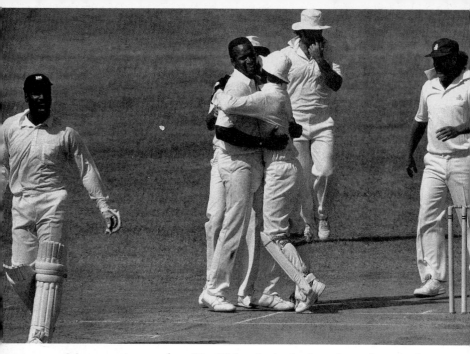

My opposite number, Viv Richards, looks less than pleased after Devon Malcolm had trapped him lbw for 21 during the West Indies' first innings in the Jamaica Test.

Another West Indies wicket goes – and don't we look happy as Carlisle Best is caught behind by Jack Russell off David Capel's bowling.

It's a double celebration for Allan Lamb in Jamaica. He does like to make the most of everything – first he celebrates his 99 (the scoreboard had got it wrong) and then comes the real thing in a marvellous century in the first Test!

It's all over! Wayne Larkins and Alec Stewart take the winning run off Ian Bishop to bring the Jamaica Test to an unbelievable climax.

Four heroes – and me! A can of beer goes down especially well for the guys who did more than most to win the first Test – Devon Malcolm, Gus Fraser, Allan Lamb and Gladstone Small.

get an early taste of some of the quality we would come up against.

There were some good signs in these games, though. Among the bowlers Phil DeFreitas picked up four wickets in the first and Gladstone Small dropped into the groove without too much trouble in the second. The one I was worried about was Devon Malcolm. He is fast – there's no doubt about that – but he was having problems with his control and it was very hard to set a field for him. He was bowling far too many bad balls, and I knew the top West Indies batsmen would never let him get away with that. At this point in the tour I knew all the bowlers had a lot of work to do; but if Dev's form didn't improve rapidly I was afraid he wouldn't make the grade.

Taken all round, however, that first week in Barbados went well, off the field as well as on it. I had a chance down on the beach to polish up my boogie boarding skills, where you lie on a small surf board, with one arm held by a thong, and you propel yourself wherever the currents – and some of them are very strong – take you.

During these first days, however, one incident brought home to me the danger that everyone in the Caribbean faces from the problem of drugs. A group of three or four lads came up to me on the beach and offered me drugs – quite openly. They were doing the same to any likely looking tourist, and they said they could get me anything I wanted. It didn't take long to convince them I wasn't interested, but I was shocked at how open they were about it all. It's a sign of the times, I suppose, but it's not something I can even start to understand.

From Barbados we went to St Kitts, where we had a four-day game against the Leeward Islands. St Kitts is a beautiful island, and the Fort Thomas Hotel where we stayed stands high on the cliffs overlooking the blue Caribbean, with the cricket ground only a mile or so away. The hospitality was brilliant, and in the first innings of our game Wayne Larkins and Alec Stewart each made good centuries, Robin Smith made 71 and Nasser Hussain 42 in our total of 444 for six. I scored 46 and I felt quite happy, though I would have liked a bit longer in the middle at this early stage of the tour. Rob Bailey was the only one to miss out. He was out for 1, and I stuck him in at number three in the second innings; but he made only 10. With just a couple of warm-up matches before the internationals started, it was going to be very hard for anyone to force their way in if they didn't make some runs early on.

On the second day we had our first look at Richie Richardson, who was leading the Leeward Islands in the absence of Viv Richards, still recovering from a broken finger. He looked in good nick and at the end of the day was unbeaten on 81. He was out early the next morning, but we had seen enough to know what a threat he would be. He had played well against us in 1986 and he gave our bowlers an early lesson in the importance of bowling tight in these conditions. Eighty per cent of his runs came in boundaries, and he was especially severe on Keith Medlycott, our slow left-armer, who was, not surprisingly, nervous in his first match on his first overseas tour.

Richardson and his team – notably Arthurton in the second innings – had shown our bowlers the name of the game in the Caribbean. For West Indians the best form of defence is attack, and their batsmen will have a go at you whenever they can. The only answer is to bowl on or just outside their off stump and never give them a chance to drive. Richardson, in particular, showed how they also love to cut. It seemed as good a time as any for Allan Lamb and me to have a meeting with the bowlers and talk to them about the best way to attack West Indian batsmen. We told them it was all about discipline – about consistently bowling to a line and length.

Lambie's experience is invaluable in these situations, and that is one of the reasons he was made vice-captain. (On the other hand, I have to report that even he occasionally needs someone to guide him. He managed to leave his passport behind in Barbados, and it was only through the kindness of the immigration people at St Kitts that he was allowed in. The passport eventually caught up with us – and luckily his calf muscle also continued to mend.)

There was one incident in the St Kitts game which I was glad to deal with early in the tour to let the players know where we stood. Nasser Hussain was given out lbw in the second innings and made it a little too obvious that he believed he had hit it. His behaviour was unacceptable under any circumstances. It was made to look worse by the fact that, a couple of overs before, Nasser had been given out to a 'catch' when the ball had clearly bounced before being held by silly mid-off, and Richie Richardson had asked the umpire to reverse his decision. Probably Nasser was still upset by this first 'dismissal'. Anyway, I took him for a little walk and made it clear that that sort of thing was just not on. Later I called all the team together and told them that while they were playing under me they would have to respect the decision of the umpire and abide by it, even if they didn't agree with it.

In the end that game was drawn, though at one stage the islanders were having a good stab at scoring the 402 runs we set them. Eventually they called it off at 301 for five – though if we had been batting I might have kept going a bit longer, since they still had overs in hand.

From St Kitts we flew south via Antigua to St Lucia for the game against the Windward Islands – though I very nearly didn't make it! At Antigua we all got off to stretch our legs. I had sat down in the airport terminal with a good book and I became so engrossed that, by the time I looked up, everyone else had rejoined the plane. When I charged aboard our little Dash 8 I found my seat had been allocated to a lady who had joined the flight there in Antigua. The stewardess pointed at another plane standing on the runway and suggested I waited for that one since it would be going the same way!

To the accompaniment of disgraceful merriment and jeering from my loyal team-mates, it was explained to her that I was the England captain and perhaps I ought to be allowed to travel with my team. Whereupon she came up with the perfect solution: why didn't Mr Larkins or Mr Smith, who were in the same row, give up his seat and travel on the other plane? In the end the problem was solved by the courtesy of the lady who had come aboard and who now volunteered to travel on the other plane.

And so we all arrived together on the beautiful, lush island of St Lucia. It was on our first day there that Ricky Ellcock had his final net and knew he would have to go home. There's not much you can say to a young lad in that situation, but I just tried to explain to him that Neil Foster had been through the same sort of problem and that after an operation he was fine. But

I don't think it cheered poor Ricky up very much at the time.

His replacement Chris Lewis arrived here in time to have two days' good practice. The choice had been between him and Glamorgan's Steve Watkin (also with the Zimbabwe party); Keith Fletcher plumped for Lewis, who is a talented all rounder. He is a lively bowler and a confident and bright character, and in general proved a good addition to the squad.

We lost by one wicket to the Windwards, and our batting suggested we could have done with an extra practice match before we met the West Indies. But that was not to be. In our first innings we were bowled out for 126 by a slow left armer named Mervyn Durand, who took seven for 15. Last summer he was playing minor league cricket in Middlesex, and he wasn't even a regular in the Windwards side. He didn't bowl quite as well as his figures suggest – our batting wasn't really up to scratch – and they hung on to some very good catches. But I was pleased with the way we fought back during their final innings, although it would have been better if we had not put ourselves in that losing situation in the first place. They needed only 136 to win, but our spinners made them struggle every inch of the way and they were nine down when they finally beat us. Eddie Hemmings and Keith Medlycott took four each, and it seemed odd that the game was dominated by spinners after so much of our pre-tour planning had concentrated on the quicker bowlers.

The really important business was due to start in Trinidad the following week with the first of the one-day internationals, so we were grateful to the Windward Islands Cricket Association for giving us a warm send-off with a reception at the Club St Lucia.

A group of holidaymakers from Essex were there and they sorted out Nasser and me at the reception. Later we returned to our hotel, where we were introduced to the local sport of hermit crab racing. This is a betting sport in which – to the surprise of some of us and to the annoyance of practically everyone – Allan Lamb proved to be an expert, to put it politely. About 10 crabs are placed in the middle of a circle drawn on the ground. In the first race you bet on which one will be the first to step outside the circle after the starter gives the 'off'. In the second race the crabs are returned to the ring and this time you bet on which crab is last to leave the circle. First of all, of course, the circle acts as the parade ring, so that everyone can examine the crabs before placing a bet in order to decide which are the liveliest and which the most lethargic. Lambie was observed by several witnesses to poke his crab gently with his finger, which made it retreat into its shell like a startled snail. This crab's thoughts were obviously going to be on other things than racing for the next few minutes, so Lambie backed it to win the second race. It duly obliged, not venturing from its shell until some time after all the other crabs had left the circle.

There were ugly mutterings of 'fix' and 'nobbling' as Lambie, who had also backed the winner of the first race, collected his pile of Eastern Caribbean dollars. But since no race steward could be found, he avoided the embarrassment of an official inquiry.

There was more entertainment when we got to Trinidad – not crabs this time, but some fun of our own making. England have a tradition that any player making his first tour has to put on some kind of show for the old hands. But we had been so busy during the Nehru Cup in India that new boys Nasser

Hussain, Alec Stewart, Robin Smith and Gus Fraser had evaded their responsibility – or so they thought. At the Trinidad Hilton we caught up with them.

Nasser, Alec and Robin each did a send-up of one of the other players, with Gus providing running commentary. It was fun, but there was a serious side to it, too: I'm sure the occasional evening like that does wonders for team spirit – though ours was running high in any case. First Nasser put on two or three pairs of glasses and took the mickey out of Devon Malcolm's fielding which, at this point, was not exactly in the Derek Randall class (although, with extra practice sessions and hard work, he was starting to show some improvement). Robin, probably because he was never going to have too much trouble with the South African accent, gave his impression of Allan Lamb's nervy, all-action lifestyle. Lambie amazes me sometimes. He can never sit still for two moments together and he always wants to be off – shopping, bargain-hunting, sight-seeing . . . you name it. Then Alec did a great skit on Wayne Larkins, who spends almost every waking hour on the phone to his lady back home.

But then came the serious business of our first visit to Trinidad: the first two Cable & Wireless one-day internationals in the series of five. Now, I regard all cricket matches as important, but none more so than internationals against another country. So it was doubly disappointing that rain interrupted both games – disappointing first because we were all looking forward to taking on the West Indies, and second because we managed only 13 overs of much-needed batting instead of the 100 we might have expected.

Before the first game we held our first serious team meeting of the tour. I emphasized the importance of being well organized and of going into the match with belief in our own ability – something I feel very strongly about and which I do all I can to instil into my teams. I believe that if you go out there looking confident and as if you mean business, it can have its effect on the opposition.

We talked about their team, which had changed a little bit (only Malcolm Marshall and Courtney Walsh of their usual squad of fast bowlers were included, and former South African rebel Ezra Moseley was back in the fold). But I didn't dwell on their side too much. I am a great believer in concentrating instead on the things you do well yourself and bringing out your individual and collective strengths.

We had proved over the past few years that we could compete on equal terms with anyone else in the world at the one-day game, and there was no reason at all why we shouldn't do well this time. We picked roughly the same team that had done well in the Nehru Cup in India, and everything was fine until about 45 minutes before the start. But then Phil DeFreitas, who has been one of our best one-day cricketers over the past few years, always bowling tight, fielding brilliantly and batting usefully at number eight, twisted his right knee in the pre-match warm-up and had to make way for Chris Lewis to make his international debut – on his 22nd birthday!

It was damp, even at the start, but I put the West Indies in when I won the toss as I felt the outfield was not wet enough to make fielding too difficult and there might be something in the pitch for the bowlers. There was a tremendous spirit among our lads as we went out to field and we bowled and fielded exactly the way we had planned. We kept the pressure on the West Indies, and even when we went through the inevitable flat spots we kept going, which is essential. It paid dividends, and we managed to restrict them to 208 for eight in their 50 overs – a pretty good performance, though I was hoping at one stage that we might get them out for 190. The wicket was still reasonable and with that sort of score either team could win. Chris Lewis had made a confident start to his international career, taking one for 30 in seven lively overs and coolly holding a catch at long on to dismiss Moseley.

We got off to a slow start, with Bishop and Marshall bowling excellently with the new ball. We soon lost Wayne Larkins, who was caught at second slip; but we were coming back into it and were 25 for one after 13 overs when the rain came. I was just planning to step up the pace when we had to go off. Although we hung around, hoping to resume, time was running out and the number of available overs was eventually reduced to a point where it would have been farcical to have carried on. Moreover, Vivian Richards wasn't keen on continuing. He clearly felt the conditions underfoot weren't good enough for his fielders, which is fair enough. The umpires seemed to agree and the match was abandoned late in the afternoon as a 'no result.'

It was blow to all of us, not least of all to the fans back in England who must have been looking forward to some live cricket on television in the middle of winter. But that's how it goes – even in the sunny Caribbean! And the next game, which we were due to play after two days' practice, was also messed up by the weather. We kept the same side as before, which meant that Chris Lewis retained his place, even though DeFreitas was making progress after his knee injury.

I won the toss again and fielded again: the pitch looked very similar to that used in the first game –

a little bit damp and a good wicket to bowl on. On the other hand, I was a bit concerned about conditions underfoot for the bowlers and fielders. My concern was soon justified when I went full length on my backside when merely stooping down to stop a gentle shot in the gully.

The interesting point is that, with a heavy downpour at 9.30, shortly before the start of play, Viv and I went out to have a look, and the conditions in the outfield all around the bowlers' run-ups were, in my opinion, three times worse than when the game was called off on the Wednesday. Yet the umpires wanted us to start promptly at 10 o'clock.

So a start was made. We had bowled 34 balls and they had scored 13 runs when it started to rain again, and it went on all day. So that was that. The series was 0–0 after two games, but we had at least shown we weren't the no-hopers we had been made out to be. We had given a good account of ourselves in the first match, and although there had been no chance to achieve anything in the second, we had done enough over the two days to put us in good spirits for the flight to Jamaica, where we were due to play the first Test.

That meant a four o'clock call and a quick breakfast at about 5.30 in the morning to catch the seven o'clock flight to Jamaica – apparently the only plane on a Sunday and involving a journey via Barbados, Antigua and Puerto Rico. It took over six hours and we arrived in Jamaica feeling shattered, which frankly does nothing at all for players trying to maintain peak physical condition.

I'd been to Kingston three times before – twice on England tours and once with the Young Cricketers. Each time I have stayed at the Pegasus, a very pleasant Trust

House hotel with a big swimming pool, tennis courts and a jogging track, which gave us ample opportunities for exercise.

On the evening after our arrival the British High Commission laid on a really good party for us. Unfortunately most of us were just too tired to do it justice. At about eight o'clock I found myself sitting down to some food at a table in the garden and it was all I could do to stop myself from falling asleep in the chair. We all left at about nine o'clock. I went straight to bed and was out like a light for eight or nine hours. I reckon I am as fit as I've ever been, what with our training programme and all the routines. But as you get older you can't keep going for as long as you used to. I found that pretty well every evening on tour, especially after a day's play, I was ready for bed and a good night's sleep by half-past nine.

While we're on the subject of fitness, I was amused to see that our training programme was beginning to rub off on a number of the press boys accompanying us. Every day they would be out running and some of them were very keen. It's something I'd never seen on a tour before, but I'm all for it. Some of them have been known to bend a modest elbow in the bar of an evening, but if they're up in the morning running it off, it can't do them much harm.

The joggers probably saw as much of Kingston as I did. We had been warned to be careful where we went, and not to venture out of the hotel on our own, as it could be dangerous. So about all I have seen of Kingston in four visits is the Pegasus and the cricket ground, Sabina Park.

One of the nicest things about our days in Jamaica was that the wives or girlfriends of four of the players turned up for a holiday. Wayne Larkins, Phil DeFreitas and

Keith Medlycott were three of the lucky ones, but the one who caused the most stir was Jenny Malcolm, Devon's wife. Jenny is a bubbly, cheery girl and, like Devon, she has Jamaican parents. Unlike Devon, however, she was born in England (in Bradford, I think), and although she had been back to Jamaica for holidays, this was a great chance for her to catch up with her relatives.

There have been countless arguments over the years about the value or otherwise of wives joining their husbands on tour. I have always been keen for Brenda to be with me whenever she could, and I can see nothing against it as long as the ladies don't keep their men from the business of the tour – which is not merely playing cricket but all the long hours spent in training and practising. But when you are playing at home in England it is quite normal to go home to one's wife and family after a day's play or at least at the end of a game. I think we should try to keep life on tour as near to normal as possible – though that is often far from easy.

On the other hand, another experienced international traveller, my friend Allan Border, is opposed to wives joining the Australian players on tour at any time. He thinks they upset the team spirit of the party.

Now to the first serious business of our visit to this lovely island: the three-day match against Jamaica, which would be followed three days later by the first of the five Test matches.

The main interest for me about the Jamaica game was that it was played on a strip only a few paces from the Test pitch. Since memories of the Test in 1986 were still painfully fresh, I was interested to see how it would play, because this would have a bearing on the side we picked for the Test.

The 1986 Test at Sabina Park was played on one of the quickest wickets I have seen anywhere. I think that was Patrick Patterson's first match for the West Indies, and the pitch was real flyer. Patterson and Malcolm Marshall bowled us out for 159 and 152, and we were beaten by 10 wickets. They had made the ball fly at us from just short of a length and, for one of the few times in my life, I really thought I was going to be injured. Obviously you can become somewhat apprehensive when two world-class fast bowlers are firing the ball at you on a really fast track – but this was the first time I'd ever really got the whiff of danger in the nostrils. The West Indies had the forces to exploit this wicket, and dished out a very demoralizing defeat, from which we never recovered and went on to lose the series 5–0. I was determined nothing like that would happen to an England team with me as its captain.

The ability to 'read' the probable nature and behaviour of a pitch is obviously important if winning the toss, and having the choice of whether to bat or bowl first, is going to crucially affect the outcome of the match. In England, of course, we play on the various county grounds so often during the season, year in, year out, that we get to know how most of them tend to behave; and, in any case, if a particular pitch is behaving unusually, we get to hear about it pretty quickly. But we tour the West Indies only every four years or so. You not only forget about the precise nature of a particular pitch – unless, like Sabina Park in 1986, it was particularly memorable – but, for all you know, they may now be preparing it in a different way.

In 1990, we were able to have a good pre-Test match look at Sabina Park's pitch in the game against Jamaica. We were told the pitch had been relaid since the 1986 Test, which was good news. In fact, it looked pretty much like the '86 track: the surface was shiny, glass-like, rock-hard and almost totally grassless, with small cracks that would obviously widen gradually as the match progressed. It looked to me like a good, flat batting wicket. And that is how it turned out – except for one thing: from about the middle of the second day the odd ball kept a bit low. I assume that this was a result of relaying the wicket and that some parts of the under-surface were less hard than others. But the point is, that was not something you could have predicted merely by looking at the pitch beforehand. For us, the important thing was to get to know the 'new' Sabina Park pitch. Equally important was that the Test track should behave in the same way.

In spite of the occasional low bounce, however, it was a good batting wicket – a fact confirmed by our batting performance against Jamaica and, in the Test match three days later, by Viv Richards' decision to bat when winning the toss. By contrast with Sabina's bare track, the pitch at Port of Spain was quite grassy. A green pitch contains moisture and is helpful to bowlers early on because the ball tends to seam. That's why, when we came to Trinidad for the third Test match and I won the toss, I put the West Indies in. Then, as the wicket dried out over the next day or two and was rolled, it started to become uneven and very difficult to bat on. And that illustrates another problem in assessing the pitch. I'm sure I was right to ask the West Indies to bat first in Port of Spain. But the other side of the coin was that we would have to bat last when – as in this case – the pitch unexpectedly started to break up. Then, for the fifth Test in Antigua, we had another common type of pitch on which the grass is white and dead after being rolled into the surface. The surface was smooth, flat and with an even texture. It looked to me to be the best of the lot, and that's how it turned out: a good batting pitch from which a fast bowler could extract some life if, as they say, he bent his back.

The ability to read a pitch comes only with time – and even then it's not a science but a mixture of experience and guesswork. Nowadays I'd say I'm right about 80 per cent of the time. But every now and then you get a pitch that behaves in exactly the opposite way you expect it to. The most striking example in my recent experience was a match Essex played in 1989 against Middlesex at Chelmsford. Mike Gatting and I went out to inspect it before the start. I, of course, know this pitch well – so does Gatt, come to that – and it looked to us like the usual Chelmsford pitch: flat, white, with possibly a bit of life in it for the bowlers on the first morning; which is why I put Middlesex in when I won the toss. Well, the ball bounced and seamed all over the place, as if there was two inches of grass on the wicket. I'd picked my slow bowlers, John Childs and Geoff Miller, but neither bowled a single ball in the match. We got them out twice for low scores, and we had to make only about 50 or so in our second innings. But the point is, the behaviour of the pitch surprised me just as much as it surprised Gatt.

For our match at Kingston, Jamaica had left out Patterson and Courtney Walsh – two bowlers almost certain to play in the Test – but that didn't bother me. We were more interested in having a look at the pitch and we picked our side from the players we thought were the most likely to play in the Test match.

We played Nasser Hussain as an extra batsman to give him some practice, which meant there was no place for Rob Bailey, Keith Medlycott, Phil DeFreitas or Chris Lewis. This must have been disappointing for them because they knew their chances of playing in the Test were greatly reduced if they did not play in the game leading up to to it. With an itinerary such as ours, made up almost entirely of international matches, it could be very frustrating if you were not in the side. There was a chance of going almost the whole tour without a game, which is what was happening to Bailey and Medlycott. They practised hard most days, helped and encouraged those who were playing, but almost never had a chance to show what they could do themselves. But this party had an excellent spirit and the players who were not in the team just had to keep going, keep their chins up, and be prepared to take their chance if it came.

In the end the game against Jamaica fizzled out into a fairly tame draw – not the type of match I really enjoy. But sometimes there is no alternative, short of throwing the game away, which is something I enjoy even less. At least some of us managed to spend a good while in the middle, and I was pleased to make 239 in the first innings. It's always nice to get a big score like that, though I had to retire temporarily at one stage as the heat and the humidity were giving me bouts of cramp. Whenever I go out to bat I have it in my mind to make 100, but to go on to 200 is tremendous. I'm no different from anyone else: I was very happy, I can tell you.

In many ways it was a good game for us. A number of the other guys also had some good batting practice, with Wayne Larkins hitting 124 in the second innings before retiring to give the others a go. Almost more important, we had a good look at the way the wicket was playing and found that after the first couple of days it was indeed keeping really low at times. And that gave us some useful clues on the make-up of our Test side.

4

Victory Against All Odds

I woke up on Friday, 2 March with a feeling of elation. The first Test was over and we had beaten the West Indies by nine wickets! The waiting and praying for the rain to stop on the Tuesday and Wednesday had all been worthwhile. We had not merely done what England had failed to do for 16 years, and what all the experts said we couldn't do; we had won by the sort of margin and with a measure of authority that, to be honest, were beyond my wildest dreams.

The experts had said that if we achieved a draw at Sabina Park we would have done well. In all honesty, I couldn't argue with that. My memories of the 1986 Test were still too fresh for me to be entirely certain that the good-looking wicket for the 1990 match would not also turn out to be fiery.

This time, however, we were as well prepared as a grand-prix racing car, though we would have welcomed another match in the pre-Test run-up. We picked six

batsmen, with two of them – Nasser Hussain and Alec
Stewart – making their Test debuts, and four seamers,
one of them, David Capel, being the all-rounder. We
omitted spinner Eddie Hemmings because in the Jamaica
match the ball had started to keep low for the seamers
as the game progressed and we thought they might be
more effective than Eddie. He had bowled well against
Jamaica, but he was not as likely to take wickets or to
put people around the bat and apply pressure.

The Test was a dream come true for Devon Malcolm.
He had played once for England, against Australia at
Trent Bridge in 1989. But here he was opening the
bowling in front of his own friends and relatives in his
home island of Jamaica. You can be sure he had to take
some stick from the crowd, but as Jenny, his wife, said
later, as soon as they realized he could bowl – and bowl
very quickly indeed – they really got behind him.

With only moments to go before lunch on the first
day, Dev pulled off a run-out that ended a useful
opening stand of 62 and dealt the West Indies a blow
from which they never really recovered. It was a great
moment for Micky Stewart and me. Right from the start
of the tour, we had known something would have to
be done to sharpen up Devon's fielding. But like most
fast bowlers, Dev does have a good arm – and that
was where Gordon Greenidge made his mistake as he
tried to take a second run after turning Gus Fraser
on the leg side. The ball hit Dev on the knee and
popped a couple of feet in front of him. He picked
it up almost straight away, but by then Gordon had
decided to take him on. Dev's throw, fast and flat,
came in over the stumps and Gordon was out by a
yard. That was the break we needed and we never looked
back.

It was no more than our bowlers deserved. Viv Richards had won the toss and elected to bat on a flat wicket; I would have done the same. But our four quick bowlers had stuck to their task and kept to their orders of bowling off stump or just outside. In the afternoon we kept plugging away and wickets started to fall, and after tea we simply ran through them. Dev Malcolm had Richards 1bw, and then Gus Fraser started to have the luck that had deserted him up to then. Gus had beaten the bat on quite a few occasions, and some of us thought he had had Richards caught behind before Dev got him. Never mind – by the evening the West Indies were all out for 164 and Gus had taken a career best of 5–28 – quite a performance for a man who had been worrying us a little right up to the start of the Test. Gus hadn't been happy with the way he was bowling; he felt the ball wasn't coming out of his hand in the way it should. That was why we had 14 overs at Jamaica at the end of the game earlier in the week to let Gus and Dev bowl a few overs in the middle, even though there had been no chance of a result.

That it paid off was largely owing to Fraser's determination and will to win – something he will have absorbed at Middlesex under the fighting leadership of people like Mike Gatting and John Emburey. But to take five for 28 against the West Indies on a pretty flat wicket, even though one or two did keep low, was a tremendous performance.

There were still a couple of hours left to negotiate when Wayne Larkins and I opened England's reply. But we played pretty well and I thought I was a trifle unlucky when I was caught down the leg side by wicket-keeper Jeffrey Dujon. I applied a fair amount of wood to a leg glance off Patrick Patterson and managed to divert the ball some yards down the leg side. But Dujon was standing a long way back and brought off a magnificent catch as he dived to his left.

Alec Stewart hit a couple of crisp fours to launch his career as an England batsman, but with the total on 60 he was caught at second slip. We ended a tremendous day at 80 for two. We were really in the one-pound seats, and that evening I said to Micky: 'If we are still batting by the close tomorrow, we'll have a tremendous chance of winning this match – not just competing with the West Indies, but actually beating them.'

Only once before – in the first Test at Trent Bridge in 1980 – had I been in a Test team that even looked like beating the West Indies. But now, on the second day, Allan Lamb and Robin Smith were the main characters as we set about batting the West Indies right out of this one. Lambie was magnificent. His 132 won him the Man of the Match award and nobody who saw it could ever doubt his right to stand among the great players of this present age. He is a great little fighter on the field and when he is batting he keeps up a constant patter with the fielding side, and especially their bowlers. He lives life to the full and he likes a drink and a good time. But there's nobody you would rather have on your side when the chips are down. I was very surprised to learn that this was the first hundred Lambie had made for England in a Test away from home. I hope there will be many more.

Robin Smith kept him company in a fourth wicket stand of 172 and we finished the second day just as I had told Micky I was hoping we would: still batting, and 180 ahead. It was the ideal position: the opposition knew they were almost out of the match and all they could hope for was to save it, which gave you a huge advantage when you bowl again. This would give our bowlers and the fielders a big incentive to go after the opposition for all they were worth.

But our batsmen weren't finished yet. Jack Russell found a stubborn partner in Gus Fraser and they put on another 22 runs to take our lead to 200, which was great. I never considered such a situation impossible for us, but I would never have had a bet that we would be so far in front at the end of the second day. All I had planned was to play as well as we could, take it step by step and see how it turned out. Now we knew.

The third day was every bit as good as the first two. We had to expect the West Indies to bat better than they had in the first innings, when they hadn't really been up to standard. But once again our four seamers plugged away manfully in the heat and Dev Malcolm made the vital breakthrough when he bowled Desmond Haynes for 14. Carlisle Best (64) and Viv Richards (37) staged a bit of a recovery, but Malcolm dismissed Viv for the second time in the game and then, as so often happens when you take one wicket, a number of others fell in quick succession.

At the end of the third day the West Indies were only 29 runs ahead with two wickets left. The first three days had gone almost entirely our way. Surely it couldn't go on like this – or could it? Next day (Monday) was the rest day. And for the first time there was a sign that something could still go wrong: it rained all day. All we could do was hang around the hotel and hope it would clear up by the morning. It was very frustrating.

I went to Sabina Park early the next morning, the fourth day. It was under water, and although they were mopping up it didn't look as if there would be any play before tea, if at all. The groundstaff continued to mop up all day, but they were doing it at their own speed.

Nothing seemed to happen very quickly, and though they were working at the ground all day, they seemed to have a lot of time on their hands. Their method was to work for half an hour, then they seemed to have a break. They may have known what they were doing, but it was driving us mad. We had never been in such a strong position in the four series I had played against the West Indies, yet here it was looking as if we might have it all snatched away by the weather!

It hardly rained at all on the fourth day, yet the ground was still very wet. I hung around as long as I could to see if perhaps we could squeeze in even half an hour, which would, hopefully, take us that much nearer to victory. But at about five o'clock the umpires finally said there was no chance, and the day's play was called off.

So we had only the final day to take two wickets and knock off, we hoped, a handful of runs. If we had a full day we had a marvellous chance of winning, but the ground was still wet and the danger was that, with rain still about, it would tip down during the night and disrupt the final day. People were telling us that the weather forecast for the next day was good, and that lifted our spirits. But I still found myself hardly daring to look as I drew back the curtain at ten past six on the morning of that final day ... and saw the sun shining! Micky was down at the ground by seven o'clock to keep an eye on the drying-up process, and when the rest of us arrived the umpires told us that, even though it was still very slightly damp, we would start on time. I had been worried about a patch to one side of the square which had taken much more water than anywhere else. I'm not saying it was anybody's fault, but it looked as if it had been caused by accidentally allowing a big puddle of water to run off the tarpaulin cover when they removed it.

At all events we were back on course and we did indeed start on time. Their last two wickets did not last very long, adding only 11 runs and leaving us 40 to make. My one disappointment was that I was out before we won. We needed only six to win, and I would have liked to have been there when the winning run was scored, even if I didn't make it myself. But the important thing was that we had won – and in little more than three days of actual playing time. Allan Lamb summed up all our feelings when he said it was the greatest day of his cricketing life.

Although they were obviously very disappointed, Viv Richards and Clive Lloyd (the West Indies manager) were very generous in defeat and the whole attitude of their team lived up to the plans Clive and I had drawn up in London before the tour even started. At a lunch at Lord's given by Cable & Wireless, the sponsors, Clive had approached me and we fell to talking about how we could make sure the series was played in a friendly and sporting manner. Clive suggested that at the close of play every day the batting side should go into the other team's dressing room for a drink. And that was what we did throughout the Jamaica Test. We play with many of their stars in county cricket throughout our summer and, since we were to stay at the same hotels for at least three of the five Tests in the West Indies, it was good if we could all be on friendly terms.

There was the usual flood of phone calls and telegrams from home – we even had one from the Prime Minister! There was also a case of Bollinger champagne and the press bought us another of Moët et Chandon, so we had plenty to celebrate with and plenty to celebrate about!

It was good to have David Gower there in his capacity as a writer for *The Times*, and I'm sure our win did something to wipe away the memories of 1986. He enjoyed our victory and was as happy as the rest of us; for although he was not a member of the England team, he was still very much a member of the England player fraternity, and I was sure it wouldn't be long before he was back again.

Practically all the spectators on the last day were English – the locals seemed to have lost some of their appetite for it. Among them was Bill Sykes, a particular friend of mine from Portugal. Bill is a businessman who has settled in the Algarve and Brenda and I have spent holidays there with him. Bill had never seen a live Test match outside England and had always promised himself that one day he would. He came all the way from Portugal to Jamaica to see this one. He certainly picked the right one! It was also good to see some of England's old stars there. Invited specially by the Jamaica Association, they were all veterans of that famous Lord's Test of 1950 – the West Indies' first victory in England. The England party included Godfrey Evans, Alec Bedser, Gilbert Parkhouse, and Hubert Doggart. But perhaps the most noteworthy guest of all was Sir Leonard Hutton, captain of the last England team to win at Sabina Park, back in 1954.

So we were one up and, as one of the journalists reminded me, I had won two of the three Tests in which I had been captain. Now the hard work would really begin. We had to continue all the good things we had been doing, in the certain knowledge that the West Indians would come back at us with everything they had – starting with the third one-day international in Jamaica on the Saturday.

5

Rain, Rain Go Away . . .

The West Indies certainly came back at us bent on revenge in the third one-day international on the Saturday after the Test. It was a fantastic game of cricket, but unfortunately we lost by three wickets – off the very last ball. Apart from us, everyone went home happy. The crowd invaded the pitch in high good spirits, and it was a welcome confidence booster for the West Indies after they had lost the first Test.

My own thoughts went back to Lord's the previous summer, when Essex lost the Benson & Hedges Cup Final to Notts off the last ball. That time, as I have said, I thought about it for three days afterwards, just wondering if I could have played it differently. But this time we had given our all. We made 214 for eight in our 50 overs, with Allan Lamb, who made 66, carrying on where he left off in the Test. It was only a moderate score, but I felt it might just be enough.

Richie Richardson hit a great 108, but the last over came with them still needing six to win and Gus Fraser to bowl it. Richardson took a single off the first, which took him away from the bowling. Ezra Moseley hit the second hard to me at short extra cover, where I was saving the one. In came Ian Bishop. Gus bowled him two dot balls, but a two to third man in between meant West Indies needed only two off the last ball to level the scores. In all the excitement we weren't quite sure what the result would be if they tied the scores. Afterwards I discovered that a tie would have been enough for the West Indies, as they had lost fewer wickets – seven against our eight.

In the event Gus didn't quite put the final ball where he wanted – it was on the off stump but slightly overpitched – and Bishop hit it through extra cover for four. So we lost. But you have to lose sometimes and we had not been outplayed: they simply nipped in at the end of one of the best games of the tour.

I enjoy the one-day matches. Of course, you can have some bad games, but the one in Kingston meant I had been involved in two really marvellous matches in eight months – the B & H final, and now this one.

The day after the one-day international we set off on another of the long, tiring journeys that are a part of touring. Yet this time I had to ask myself whether it was all really necessary. Our eventual destination was Guyana, where we were due to play the second Test. But since there are no flights directly from Kingston to Georgetown, the capital of Guyana, we had to go back to Trinidad and spend the night there. Once again we had to repeat the process of calling at Puerto Rico, Barbados and Antigua on the way, and we didn't arrive in Trinidad until late at night – at least 11 hours door-to-door from Kingston. The travelling on tours is considerable – often people don't realize how much of it there is – and a trip like that really takes it out of a player who has been on the field in the heat only the day before. There were 20 in our party, almost as many in the West Indies squad, who were on the same plane, plus 70 or more press, photographers, radio and TV people. I can't understand why the West Indies Board couldn't charter an aircraft from BWIA (British West Indian Airways) to take us directly to Guyana without all the complications.

As it was, some of the press found their flight from Trinidad in the morning hopelessly overbooked and BWIA had to put some of them up in the Hilton Hotel until the next day. And then, with all the confusion, something like 21 bags were mislaid, including those belonging to Viv Richards and Clive Lloyd. Tours are tough enough without unnecessary hassle, and I would have thought it was at least worth looking into the question of chartering aircraft when so many people are involved, instead of relying on busy and often overbooked scheduled flights. It's not a problem that occurs on tours of England, of course. But in Australia, Ansett Airlines are given a free plug every time Channel 9 cover cricket. With a bit of imagination I'm sure we could do the same.

Eventually we reached Guyana in a fair state of exhaustion. It was no way for professional sportsmen to travel unless it was completely unavoidable – and in this case I'm sure something could have been done to make our journey easier. Micky Stewart said that when he arrived he sat down to write a letter, but he was so exhausted he couldn't even start. I'm sure a lot of us know how he felt.

At least Guyana didn't appear as bad as we had been led to believe. We had heard there were a lot of shortages and that everyday things like bread and even toilet rolls were hard to come by. So a lot of the lads had stocked their suitcases in Jamaica with biscuits, cheese and that sort of thing.

I had stayed at the Pegasus Hotel in Georgetown before when I came on the 1981 tour – the time we were all deported because of the Robin Jackman affair. I remembered that the hotel had been friendly and helpful and gave us all we needed, so I wasn't unduly worried. Guyana is a very poor country. The present government is working hard to repair some of the damage caused by the previous extreme left-wing regime of Forbes Burnham, but it is a long haul. They have no foreign currency, so they can't import anything. All foreign firms have departed and the exchange system is conducted either by your taxi driver or by street dealers, who operate quite openly in America Street (or Wall Street, as it is known locally).

But there are compensations. The people were among the friendliest we had met anywhere and they couldn't do enough for us. The food was OK and all the precautions the lads had taken were unnecessary. There was only one little matter that really bugged us, and there wasn't much we could do about that: the weather.

It rains a lot in Georgetown, situated as it is on the South American coast, with tropical rain forests to the south and the Atlantic Ocean to the north. Much of coastal Guyana is some five feet below sea level and is protected along its length by a sea wall built by the Dutch when they occupied the place. So it is more than just a joke when they say in Guyana that all you have to do to make it rain is to put up two sets of stumps!

In 1981 we never even had time to put the stumps up before the Jackman row burst around our ears, yet there was so much rain that year that I don't think the Test match would have been possible anyway. But I had played at Bourda when the England Young Cricketers toured in 1972; and all seemed set fair this time when we met the West Indies in the fourth one-day international.

After losing the third game in Jamaica, I was keen to get our winning momentum going again as I am a great believer in the importance of developing a winning habit. It makes it more likely you'll win if you go on the field believing you are going to be successful. So at the team meeting the night before I told the lads how important this game was and that it was imperative for them to play their best. We had proved we were a match for the West Indies, but that would count for nothing if we became complacent and assumed it was all going to happen for us.

At Bourda on Wednesday we found out just how true that was. We didn't play at all well and we lost by six wickets. It was disappointing for me, but the defeat served to drive home the point I had been trying to make – that we had to maintain our attitude and our application throughout the tour.

We had to realize that at Bourda that day we had one of the little setbacks that a young and inexperienced side is bound to have on occasion. We made only 188 on a flat pitch where you would normally be looking for something like 230 or 240. It took the West Indies until the second over from the end to make the runs, but they had lost only four wickets, with Carlisle Best making a brilliant hundred.

Unfortunately there wasn't much chance of improving our cricket during the remainder of our stay in Guyana. It started raining the day after the one-day international and didn't stop long enough for the ground to dry out until the Test match was almost due to end. We had been told when we arrived that the forecast wasn't too good for the Test. Apparently it usually rains at the time of the full moon – and the moon was full on the Sunday, the second day of the Test. The days were usually quite bright and humid – but every night and early morning it tipped down. I don't think I've ever seen a cricket ground quite as wet as Bourda that week. The ditches around the ground that are supposed to carry the water away were overflowing and the outfield was under several inches in places.

It was said that the drains were blocked and the water wasn't running away into the canals the way it should. All I know is that I never even had a good look at the pitch as it was mostly under water.

This was a great disappointment to us all because, although we were one up in the series, none of us wanted to hide behind behind the rain and use it as a way to maintain our lead. We wanted to go out there and play and, if we could, do even better than we had done in Jamaica.

We did get as far as picking a team – the same 12 that were on duty in Jamaica – but that was about all we could do. The only slight problem, strangely enough, concerned myself, though I would have played if the Test had ever started. I had two boils on my left thigh that seemed to be a hangover from our Nehru Cup trip to India, where I developed a similar boil on my face. It was obviously something that had got into my blood, and when I arrived back from India I had visited Tony Hall, a specialist in tropical medicine, at his Wimpole Street clinic. He had gone with us to the World Cup a year earlier and had been a big help in keeping everyone up to scratch.

I know that Laurie Brown, our physio, was relieved that I didn't have to play for at least the first couple of days in Guyana, as the boils would have caused me some discomfort, especially if my leg became hot and sweaty under the thigh pad. Laurie has been a boon to the English team ever since he took over the physio's job from Bernie Thomas for the 1986 tour of the West Indies. That was a tough tour to have as your first trip – especially as up to then Laurie had been more involved with soccer than cricket, having worked for Wolverhampton Wanderers and then Manchester United. Laurie reckons that in 1986 he was on the field almost as much as the players as we took a bit of a battering from some of their fast bowlers – though his worst moment came when Dennis Waight, the Aussie physio with the West Indies team, collapsed in the dressing room at Barbados with kidney trouble. Laurie had to decide whether he could be spared from the ground long enough to go to hospital with Dennis, giving him oxygen in the ambulance as they rushed him to hospital.

We were hoping nothing as serious would happen on this tour. But there were moments in Guyana when Laurie's humour and ingenuity were stretched to the limit just to keep us from going mad from boredom and inactivity. Some days we could hardly venture outside because of the rain. There was virtually no practice, either for us or the West Indies, who were also staying at the Pegasus. There's no shortage of cricket grounds in Guyana, but they were all under water as well; even the concrete nets and their surrounds were flooded.

Some days we ran on the sea wall. Other times we jogged to a nearby park where we did some sprinting, and sometimes we played indoor football at Guyana's National Sports Hall, where they had a local coach called Willy who became very friendly and helpful to me. I would do weight training and sit ups, which I enjoy, and on occasions Graham Morris, one of the photographers in the party, and Robin Smith would join me.

I carry a set of bar bells around with me on my travels, and Robin and Jack Russell were often keen to join in with me. There was also a tennis court at the Pegasus, which we put to all sorts of uses. Just to keep the feel of a bat in my hands I would go there and ask people like Peter Lush, the tour manager, or even some of the press boys, to throw balls at me.

That court did at least provide the only matches between England and the West Indies that ever looked like taking place: several of their players, including Viv Richards, took some of our lads on at tennis. I think they usually won, too! But the court also provided one mishap – and caused Laurie Brown a lot of extra worry. Nasser Hussain was playing tennis when he slipped and injured his left wrist quite badly. Though it seemed to recover well, Nasser's wrist was still not fully fit for the third Test in Trinidad, which meant he reached Barbados at the end of March not having played at all since the first Test over a month earlier. That is far from the sort of preparation he needed for whenever he would be called upon, but it couldn't be helped.

One of the problems of a tour like this one to the West Indies is that there are now very few games outside the Tests and one-day internationals in which to give everyone a game. Somebody is always going to miss

Trust Allan Lamb not to get his feet wet, even if he is the one wearing the flip-flops! Still, I reckon those two lads have found the right gear for watching cricket in Guyana.

The pitch at Bourda looks a bit on the damp side – but Nasser Hussain, Alec Stewart, Phil DeFreitas and Robin Smith are determined to have a game of some sort.

Alec Stewart and Nasser Hussain find the only way to get a cricket bat in their hands in Guyana is to play tennis with it on the hotel courts – the same place where Nasser later injured his wrist.

Allan Lamb leads the physical jerks on the sea wall that is meant to keep the Atlantic Ocean out of Guyana. Sometimes we wondered if it was working!

Time to stop and think with manager Micky Stewart on the Georgetown sea wall – but what about? Those clouds in the background say it all – no play today!

Gus Logie forces one away off the back foot during the first West Indies innings in the Trinidad Test. He was definitely more sorry than we were when Allan Lamb caught him at slip off Gus Fraser for 98!

Jack Russell takes a throw-in as Gus Logie makes room.

Logie again – this time he's about to catch Rob Bailey.

No doubts for Allan Lamb and Gus Fraser as they shout for lbw against Gordon Greenidge in the second innings at Port of Spain.

Jack Russell is the centre of attention again after catching Richie Richardson in the first innings at Port of Spain.

Now just you look here! Desmond Haynes makes his point not long before I was injured.

Ouch! This was the worst moment of the tour for me. The ball flies off on the leg side – via my left hand – after it was hit by Ezra Moseley in the second innings at Port of Spain.

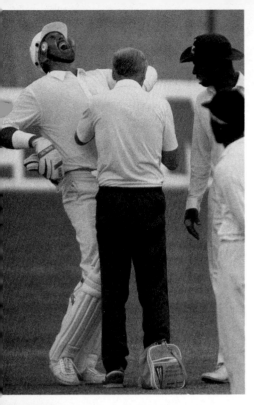

Does that hurt? Laurie Brown tries a spot of first aid on my damaged hand – but there was little he could do. It was broken and I was out of the rest of the tour.

Ted Dexter looks suitably concerned as our chances of winning the Trinidad Test slip away.

out. Early on in this tour it was Rob Bailey, and later it was Keith Medlycott and Chris Lewis. As captain I was always aware that any one of those players might suddenly be called upon, and an unexpected injury, like the one that had just befallen Nasser, only served to highlight that fact.

We were lucky that all the players had such a positive attitude and there was never a hint of heads dropping. Even so, from time to time I felt it right to take the unlucky ones who weren't playing much cricket to one side and have a chat with them. I wanted them to know they were as important to the tour as those who were playing regularly and that their chance would come. They all accepted the situation cheerfully and that helped keep up the spirits of the party. Keeping up everyone's spirits was one of the main tasks in Guyana. We found a restaurant near the hotel called La Casa and we used to go there most nights – it made a change from hanging around one's room or the hotel lobby.

By the rest day it was becoming clear there would not be any chance of a meaningful Test match, so we suggested to the West Indies Board that perhaps we could go to Trinidad and play a couple of one-day games there. We were beginning to run out of ideas of how to pass the time and we thought that some cricket in Trinidad might be the answer. But there were problems in arranging the move and the people in Guyana seemed keen to give the weather every chance to improve.

So trips were organized to some of the places of interest in the interior. Some of the guys took a plane ride to the Kaieteur Falls, reckoned to be one of the highest waterfalls in the world. On the Sunday the hotel manager took me, Allan Lamb, Gladstone Small and Robin Smith for a trip up the Demerara River, which comes out into the sea at Georgetown. We sailed about a mile up the river in this little ski boat before turning off into a narrow creek which carved its way deep into the dark, green jungle. It was just like a scene out of one of David Attenborough's nature programmes on TV as we chugged through the black water, with the vines and creepers dangling into the boat and shutting out almost all the light overhead.

About three miles up the creek we came to an Amerindian village, where all the children were paddling back from school in their little dugout canoes. The hotel manager was building a weekend cottage in the village and I could see it would make an exciting holiday spot for anyone with a sense of adventure. The trip succeeded in passing the time agreeably enough. But there still wasn't any cricket.

Eventually, on the Tuesday (which had been specified as the rest day) the West Indies decided to call off the Test. It was agreed to play a one-day international on each of the last two days – the Wednesday and the Thursday. But though the weather was better, we didn't think the ground would be fit for the Wednesday, so we suggested we play one single innings match on the Thursday.

That set something of a precedent as the Thursday had been scheduled to be the last day of the Test and we would be playing a one-day international instead. But I didn't feel it would be very meaningful to play just one day of a Test, and it would be better for the fans and for all concerned if we played a complete one-day match that day, which we did.

In the event, we lost heavily and deserved to. The match was played not on the pitch used for the fourth one-day international but on the one that would have been used for the Second Test. This, of course, had been covered for several days, and so it was decidedly sporting for the first few hours of play. All in all it was a very good toss to win. Jeff Dujon, who captained the West Indies in the absence of Richards, Haynes, Logie and Marshall, won the toss and put us in. We managed only 166 for nine off 49 overs – something less than 3.5 runs an over – and in his first opportunity to bowl against us on this tour, Curtly Ambrose took 4 for 19 in nine overs. The encouraging thing from our point of view was Rob Bailey's nicely made 42 in his first innings for six weeks; this, in view of Nasser Hussain's injury, was a good omen.

By the time the West Indies went in the pitch had flattened out quite a bit and they made the runs comfortably with only three wickets down. It was only an unofficial one-day international, but there was no getting away from the fact that we had lost our momentum. It was up to us to find it again in Trinidad as we approached the third Test in Port of Spain.

6

Pain and Despondency

Our flight out of Guyana was a lot more comfortable than the journey in. I'm not certain whose idea it was – perhaps it came from BWIA – but our whole party, including the West Indian players and the press, were given a DC-9 of our own to take us to Trinidad.

We sailed through immigration at Timehri, the main airport, south of Georgetown, and had no hassles on arrival at Port of Spain. No bags were lost, there was no waiting, and we all arrived reasonably fresh. This really is the way travel should be conducted on tours, and I hope the authorities will bear this in mind in the future.

Our first game in Trinidad was against the West Indies Board President's team at a ground called Guaracara Park at Pointe-à-Pierre, a small town some 40 miles south of Port of Spain. That meant a one-hour drive from the Trinidad Hilton as there are no hotels in Pointe-à-Pierre, so we were making an early start and a late finish – nearly a 12-hour day. But we were well looked after at Guaracara Park, which is right in the middle of an oil terminal – the third largest in the world, I'm told. That is where most of Trinidad's wealth is generated; the only problem is that there is always an acrid smell coming from the refinery. Most of us were unaffected, but Eddie Hemmings, who suffers from asthma, found breathing difficult at times.

The four-day game went reasonably well, and we won by 113 runs on the last day. The game ebbed and flowed a bit and at one stage we were in trouble. At the start of the last morning we were only 93 in front with four wickets left. Rob Bailey had made 52 in the first innings, his second good score of the week, and that had put him in the running for a place in the side for the third Test, especially as Nasser Hussain's wrist was still painful and he had to miss this game at Guaracara Park. On the last morning the pitch was showing signs of deteriorating quite rapidly, but Robin Smith, with some help from Jack Russell and Phil DeFreitas, made a superb 99 before he ran out of partners. Given the conditions it was a marvellous innings and a welcome return to form for him.

Robin is an extremely talented player. He has all the courage and determination that we see in many South African cricketers, and he is always looking to dominate the bowling. But on this tour we had come up against some tricky pitches and, on the advice of several older heads, including Geoff Boycott, who was here with Sky Television, Robin curbed some of the shots that might bring four but might also cost him his wicket.

I hit 60-odd in each innings and I thought I was really playing well. I was disappointed not to make a hundred in at least one of those knocks: I made just two mistakes

in the whole game and I was out both times, both to
Robert Haynes, a tall leg spinner from Jamaica who
took eight wickets in the match. Haynes is a tall man
and relies on bounce as much as spin, but he can also bat
and I would not have been surprised if the West Indies
had chosen him for the third Test.

The highest score of the match was the 134 made in
their first innings by young Lara, a player we had not
seen before, who could well be a name to watch. A
wristy player who strokes the ball around, his technique
reminds me not so much of West Indian batsmen as of
some of the more accomplished Pakistanis.

In the end we bowled them out in their second innings
for 123, which was the perfect boost for the Trinidad
Test. All our bowlers performed well. There was also
a bit of fun regarding a security guard and his German
Shepherd dog. Time and again play at one end had been
held up as people wandered to and fro in front of the
sight screen. So this guard stationed himself beside the
screen with his dog tied on a leash just long enough for
it to reach anyone who ventured past the screen at the
wrong time. From that moment on nobody risked it!

When we arrived back at the Trinidad Hilton after the
game on Monday (the third day of the match), we found,
among the many British supporters who were turning up
for the Test, Colin Tomlin and his wife Carol. Colin was
the man Micky Stewart had pulled in to help co-ordinate
the England party's fitness programme before we left for
the West Indies. He had become very popular with the
lads and we were pleased to have him there. Colin is an
athletics coach who comes from Canterbury. He is mad
keen on English cricket and English sport in general,
and I was quick to enlist his help with the Essex team's
preparations for the 1990 season. He will be good for

Essex. He gees the boys up and puts them in the right frame of mind, and I hope he remains involved with the England team. He is a quiet chap and he told me he was quite nervous on his first day with us, wondering how he was going to shout at people like me and Allan Lamb. But he soon found we were keen to listen and do what he said, and it all developed from there.

He taught us all a lot about fitness – in fact he had to tell me to ease off once or twice. I am always keen to run and train as hard as I can, but Colin made it clear to me that sometimes you have to take it easy.

It was now the day before the third Test – the game I regarded as the crucial match of the series. With us having won one and with one having been rained off, we were in the position that if we either won or drew this Test, the West Indies would go into the last two Tests knowing they had to win them both either to take the series or to square it. Obviously, if we won the third Test, then they would have to win the last two merely to level the series, and that would be a fantastic position to be in. I would certainly have settled for that before we left England.

The West Indies were without their captain Vivian Richards, who had a recurrence of his haemorrhoids problem. I think this was the first time I had played against a West Indies side without Viv in it. They were going to miss his experience – and, of course, his batting. They were also without Malcolm Marshall, another of their most experienced players, who had broken his finger in the first Test when Allan Lamb hit one back at him. They brought in Ezra Moseley to replace Marshall in their 13, and Gus Logie came in for Richards after missing most of their season with a hand injury.

Logie had skippered the President's team against us at Guaracara Park and both Micky Stewart and I noticed how well he did with his field placings and bowling changes. But Desmond Haynes was appointed captain for the Test – the first time he had led the West Indies, so it would be a big match for him too. They also brought in Brian Lara, the little left-hander who had batted very well and made a hundred against us at Guaracara Park. He was only 20 and I didn't expect him to play just yet.

We had a couple of injury problems ourselves to sort out before we could name our side. Nasser Hussain was still feeling slight twinges in his wrist; besides, he hadn't played for more than a month. And Allan Lamb had missed the match at Guaracara Park with a bruise on the inside of his right thigh. But omitting him for that game was more of a precaution than anything else, and I was confident he would be fit.

The Test itself was crucial, sometimes controversial and, in the end, bitterly disappointing. In short, it had just about everything except the right result for us. It was one of the best Tests I have ever played in, gripping all the way through, especially on the last couple of days – and right up to the final ball. So much happened, in fact, that the only way to remember it all is to go through it blow by blow. And when I say blow, that's exactly what I mean, since in this game, on that eventful last day when probable victory turned into a disappointing draw, I broke my hand for the first time in my career. What a time to do it!

As expected, Nasser Hussain was not fit, and Rob Bailey came into the side at number six. Apart from that, we went in with the same team that had won in Jamaica. I was sorry not to have Nasser in the side as he had looked promising in Jamaica, but at the same time it was good to give Bailey a chance; he had not had many opportunities on the trip up to that point. It was a great shame that, as things turned out, he bagged a pair in the Test. I know how he felt – the same thing happened to me in my first Test, against Australia at Birmingham in 1975. This wasn't Rob's first Test, of course. He had played once before, in the game at The Oval against the West Indies in 1988 when I took over the captaincy for the first time. I don't suppose he would have played in this one if Nasser had been fit, but it was such a shame that Rob was out to two nasty deliveries – one lifted and he nicked it to short leg, while the other one kept low and he was bowled. But Bailey had been a tremendous tourist. He accepted his lot very well, he kept his spirits up, and his attitude was first rate all through. That's hard to achieve when you're not playing, and I'm sure it will not be forgotten in the future.

First things first, though – and that means the toss. It's always important to win the toss if you can, but it was never more so than in this Test. The pitch looked as if it was going to be green and favour the seam bowlers. When I played here in 1986 there was a lot more grass on it than there had been in 1981. It was the sort of wicket where you put the opposition in if you won the toss. It would be a good toss to win because I thought the pitch would be better on the second and third day, and would then become gradually more and more uneven on the fourth and final days. And that, as it turned out, was exactly right. We read the pitch pretty accurately and I was lucky enough to win the toss and put the West Indies in. When I say that 'we' read the pitch right, I mean that I talked things over with Micky Stewart and Allan Lamb; but in the end it had to be the captain's decision whether to bat or field. By and large we agreed most of the time. On some wickets it's fairly obvious what you ought to do, but on others it's purely a matter of guesswork. Usually it's best to bat in those situations, but not always.

After I had put the West Indies in, somebody – I think it was Alan Lee of *The Times* – asked me if it was because I didn't want the opposition to bowl first at us. I never think like that: that would be a defensive move. I make my decision, whether it is in county cricket or in a Test, on what is *positively* best for my side. In other words, my decision is always based on my team's strengths, not their weaknesses. You bat or bowl simply on your opinion of the pitch and whether it would be best for batting or for bowling. Sometimes, especially in England, you have to take notice of the weather forecast as well, and if there is rain about I would usually bowl, particularly in a one-day match.

In the event, without being too smug, I think I guessed right about the wicket in Trinidad. It played as I thought it would and it's now a matter of history that, in the end, only the weather stopped us from winning. Meanwhile, the decision to bowl first was obviously the right one: the West Indies crashed to 103 for eight – though I must say I didn't think the pitch really warranted a score like that. It certainly wasn't that bad and I could hardly believe we had done so well. But everything went well – our bowlers put the ball in the right spot, we caught our catches and it was a great team performance. In the end it was very disappointing that they made 199, when at one time they looked as if they would be lucky to reach 150. But I can't be too critical – if I had been told before we started that we would bowl the West Indies out for less than 200 I would have been very, very happy. It's just that, having put them in real trouble, it was a pity we allowed them to make something of a recovery.

If we had bowled them out for less than 150 there is little doubt we would have won the game. It would have been nothing more than we deserved, since we outplayed them on every day. But our bowlers were bound to be feeling a bit tired, the ball was older, and Gus Logie played very well for his 98. He is a good little player. He's not conventional: he hits the ball late and, as if emulating the lager, he hits it to parts of the ground other players can't reach. He relies on subtlety and stealth rather than power. He's one of those guys who has 20 on the board before you know it, and he's not easy to get out. Well, Gus took his side almost to 200; without him they would have been annihilated.

When we went out to bat the one thing uppermost in my mind was to make sure we consolidated the position the bowlers had given us by batting at least until the end of the second day. I know people have said we were too slow, but I can assure you that Wayne Larkins and I didn't go out there with the intention of blocking it out. Both of us like to attack. But we knew that if we were still there at the end of the second day with wickets in hand, we would be in a very strong position. And that's how it turned out.

It was slow, but I felt it was justified: by the end of the day we were almost level with them with only two wickets down. They bowled well and some time was lost to rain, but I wasn't thinking primarily of not losing the game – I was thinking in terms of winning it. We were very cautious as I didn't want to give them any chance of finding a way back into the game after we had started so well.

We had lost a couple of hours through rain. The pitch had freshened up a bit under the covers and it certainly moved around a lot more after that. We were certainly slow – but the West Indies weren't bowling much more than 11 overs an hour at us for the greater part of the day, and there's a limit to the number of runs you can score if people aren't bowling the ball at you.

I have to admit that we were not bowling our overs much quicker than them. It disappointed me very much, and I kept trying to gee the lads up to bowl our overs at around 15 an hour. But with the drinks breaks, two of them in the afternoon, plus a few wickets, you can lose over 20 minutes. I don't think two drinks breaks are necessary. And I'm not blaming their batsmen for our over rate, but they do mess around somewhat between overs.

There was supposed to be a minimum of 90 overs a day in this series; but there was no way it could be achieved unless you bowled the spinners. I think it's a good idea to try and bowl that number of overs, but to do so we were having to carry on for at least another half an hour until the light became too bad to go on any longer.

The Test started to even out a bit on the third day when they dismissed us for 288, which gave us a lead of 89. We would have liked it to have been more, but things didn't go quite so well for us and they started to bowl well, so you have to give them credit. At the end of the day they had eight overs to bat: a situation in which the batsmen are on a hiding to nothing. I've had to do it any number of times myself; and nobody likes it. You know you have to survive eight overs, you aren't going to make many runs, but you can get out. The thing we didn't want was to give them a chance to come off for the light, which was becoming quickly worse. So, in hindsight, I wish I hadn't given Devon Malcolm the new ball. Devon had come on well on this tour. He was willing to learn and was keen. He was also quick – as quick as anybody in the West Indies team – and in the Trinidad match, when some of them did not quite put things together, he was the quickest bowler of all. And the West Indies knew that, believe me.

At the end of the third day, however, Devon bowled one bouncer to Gordon Greenidge, and that was it: the umpires offered them the light and they were off – which seemed a bit strange to me, as the West Indies had been bowling bouncers to Devon when the light was every bit as bad and the umpires had made no offer to him. As we went off I must admit I thought I had made a mistake in allowing Devon to take the new ball with Gladstone Small. Of course, eventually he ended up with 10 wickets and the Man of the Match award, which he fully deserved. But at that point it might have been better to give the ball to Gus Fraser, who would have been sure to put it there or thereabouts and we would have had the full eight overs at them, with the chance of picking up a wicket.

I told Devon to keep the ball up, but he still didn't have the greatest control, even though he was improving all the time. Unfortunately he overdid it and gave Gordon two friendly half volleys, which he hit through mid-off for four. When he tried to put that right and bowl a bit shorter, he overdid it again and bowled a bouncer which hit Greenidge on the helmet and went for four leg byes.

So, Greenidge and Desmond Haynes survived the final session and by lunch on the fourth day they had cleared the arrears without loss. Soon afterwards, however, we made the breakthrough when Gus had Greenidge lbw.

And then, as so often in Test cricket – or in any sort of cricket, come to that – several others fell.

It was Devon Malcolm who did the business. The wicket seemed to have eased a little at this point, but in a single over he nipped out three of them – Desmond Haynes, Carlisle Best and Jeff Dujon. With the total on 100 we were back in the driving seat, a just reward for sticking it out and raising our game when things seemed to be going against us. They had only one wicket left when the last day began. We took that fairly swiftly and they were all out for 239, leaving us to make 151 to win and go two up in the series.

If only it had been that simple! The wicket had deteriorated by then, with some balls jumping off a length and some shooting through low. But one bonus for us was that the West Indies did not bowl as well as they can. Almost from the start of our innings they dropped the ball too short when, if they had bowled on a length, they would have had every chance of making one either shoot or rise sharply – which is what happened to me in the end!

By bowling short on this kind of wicket you give the batsman that extra fraction of a second to react to an abnormal bounce. We managed to get away to a good start, and at lunch we were 70 for one. Apart from being a great position statistically – only 81 more runs needed – it was also good from a psychological point of view. By then I had already gone off with a broken hand, but Allan Lamb and Alec Stewart were in a good, positive frame of mind and going well, while the West Indies looked as if they were down. I'm sure that if we had been able to carry on immediately after lunch we would have won – not comfortably, because it was a very dodgy wicket by then, but with something in hand.

But it was not to be: the rains came and we lost three hours at a critical point. I know it happens all the time – it's very much part of the game. But this time it came almost to order for the West Indians, at the very moment when we were about to make cricket history.

When we eventually re-started after the rain we knew the West Indies were not going to bowl a lot of overs. There were officially 30 overs remaining, and with the light fading we thought we might have 20 of them. As it turned out they only bowled 16, and we eventually came off at about six o'clock with five wickets down and only 30 runs short of our target.

The reason we came off was that I didn't think they would be able to bowl three or four overs in the next 20 minutes, and by 6.15 or 6.20 it was going to be almost pitch dark. I was going in next with my broken hand and what we didn't want to do was to risk possible defeat. If we had lost another wicket we would have been six down when I went in. If something went wrong and either I found I couldn't bat at all or else I was out, our tail would have been exposed to the West Indies bowlers in very poor light. They could conceivably have stolen the match, which they wouldn't have deserved.

I wasn't about to let them back into the series in those conditions. If we had had three wickets down or less we might have kept going for another 10 minutes. But really it wasn't feasible to score 30 runs in three or four overs on a dodgy pitch in bad light. So we called off the chase. It has been suggested we should have gone on for another couple of overs and then accepted the light if anything went wrong. But the umpires had already offered us the light and I was afraid it might not get any worse in the time left. And if it didn't, the umpires might not have given us another chance.

Carlisle Best on his way to 164 in the Barbados Test.

Didn't he do well? Best and friends celebrate his Barbados century.

David Gower practises in Barbados – but in the end he wasn't needed.

Nasser Hussain hooks Curtly Ambrose in England's first innings.

Viv Richards raises his finger – and so does the umpire, Lloyd Barker, to signal the end of Robert Bailey's second innings in Barbados.

The start of the trouble. Robert Bailey is caught by Jeff Dujon, but did he hit it?

David Smith's only innings is over – bowled by Ezra Moseley for five in the Barbados one-day international.

Share and share alike – that's the motto for Allan Lamb and Robin Smith as they fight to save the fourth Test.

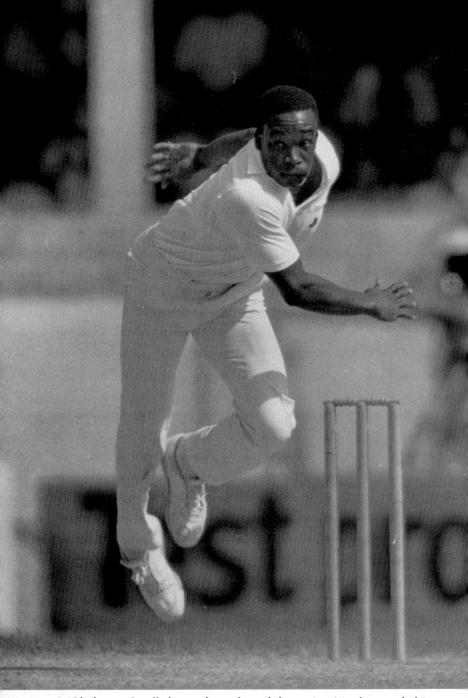

Gladstone Small shows the style and determination that made him our second highest wicket-taker in the Tests with 17 victims at 29.70 apiece. Only Devon Malcolm took more — he had 19 at 30.36.

I felt that by then we had done all that could be expected of us. Alec Stewart, in particular, and Allan Lamb, had batted well and there's no doubt they had the West Indies worried. Alec was playing well in the last innings. He was doing the right thing – playing his shots on a very unpredictable pitch – and he was unlucky to be out the way he was, caught at third man off one that he hit off the middle of the bat.

At one point there was an extended 'conversation' between Alec and Desmond Haynes. A lot was made of this by the media because it was so visible to the crowd and the television audience. Haynes was fielding close to the bat and he would walk right up to Alec and they would exchange a few words more or less eyeball to eyeball, after which Haynes would return to his position. I don't know if Haynes was over-tense – worried, perhaps, that he might lose his first Test as captain. At all events, Alec is the wrong man to attempt to 'influence' in this way: he is a veteran of grade cricket in Australia, where 'sledging' is part and parcel of the game. It was all pretty trivial, I'm sure the two players were equally responsible, and I would not raise the matter here if the press hadn't got so excited by it.

Alec had been a bit short of runs before the Trinidad Test, but that happens to most of us at some time. He was in the unique position on this tour, of course, in that his father was the manager. But if you had seen them or listened to them, you would never have guessed it: they were both so aware of the situation that, rather than appear to be too close, they behaved with considerable formality to each other in public.

Let's not forget David Capel's contribution to this match. He batted well, with a lot of determination, to make 40 and 17 not out. He's a good cricketer, though he's still finding his feet at Test match level. He has improved a lot on this tour, especially in his bowling. When he runs in he can be quite quick – not all the time, but with the odd ball – and his accuracy has improved. And he has got stuck in with the bat. They were a couple of good knocks in Trinidad – and not on the easiest of wickets, either.

I, of course, have pretty mixed feelings about the pitch at Port of Spain. It was mainly responsible for breaking my left hand in two places and putting me on the sidelines for the remainder of the tour. Not only that, my injury must have played a big part in preventing us from winning a Test that we had dominated.

I had been playing pretty well, had made 18 and was feeling good. Then I received these two balls from Ezra Moseley, who was the quickest of the West Indian bowlers in this match. They were good-length balls that simply flew off one of the cracks in the pitch. They weren't bouncers, as was falsely reported in some of the papers – just good-length balls that reared up.

The first one hit me as I moved back to play a defensive shot. It struck the top of my left hand and went down to the bat and pad position. We took a single as Wayne Larkins was coming for the run. The hand was already hurting badly, but I could still just about hold the bat and carry on. The very next time I went down to Moseley's end the same thing happened again. The ball pitched in the same spot, I went back again and the ball leapt up and hit me in exactly the same place. That finished me off.

I'm used to being hit on the hands, but I've never broken a finger before, and I wasn't fully aware of what had happened. I couldn't hold the bat at all and I thought at first that it was a dislocation as the small knuckle on my left hand was depressed. It was obvious I couldn't go on as it was. Laurie Brown, our physio, tried to pull it back into position, which was simply agony.

I've gone through my entire career, some 17 years, without ever missing a game for Essex or England through injury. I've had a few dislocated fingers and chipped bones, but never enough to keep me out. This one couldn't have happened at a worse time, as we were well on our way to victory. I went for an X-ray at St Clare's Medical Centre at lunch-time and they confirmed that it was broken in two places. We asked the doctors to keep it to themselves and just say that it was badly bruised. And that was how we put it to the media, because it was obvious that, if I needed to bat again – and there was every chance I would – I didn't want the West Indies to know that the hand was broken; it might have given them that extra boost at a time when the tide was running against them.

During the stoppage for rain Jeff Dujon, their wicket-keeper, came into our dressing room to ask me how I was. I had the feeling he was there to discover, if possible, whether I was in a fit state to bat. I was very polite, thanked him for asking, and said it was only bruised and that I would be batting later if needed.

After the match I went back to the Medical Centre for an operation which lasted an hour. They numbed my arm with a local anaesthetic and put two wires through the broken bone and into the next joint in the adjoining finger to lock it like a splint. These wires, they told me, would have to stay in for at least two weeks, which not only put me out of all the matches in Barbados, including the Test, for sure, but also made me doubtful for the final Test in Antigua.

7

West Indies Hit Back

Our main worry as we left Trinidad and headed to Barbados for the fourth Test was our ever-lengthening injury list – a problem that eventually proved almost too much to overcome. The first hurdle to be faced was the three-day game against Barbados, which started the day after we arrived on the island.

I was obviously out of that one with the injury I'd received in Trinidad and we were still having trouble with Nasser Hussain's wrist, although it was only later, after we had arrived in Antigua, that it was confirmed that it was in fact broken, not sprained as we had originally believed.

Our first task was to find a replacement opening batsman, since we had only brought two – myself and Wayne Larkins. That was a deliberate policy decision, as we knew we could fall back on Alec Stewart; and that is what we did for the match against Barbados. I would have preferred to call in a specialist opener, though, and that was why, in the end, we sent home for David Smith of Sussex. But there was no way he could arrive in time for the match against Barbados, so we had to do something about that – and quick!

For later matches, quite a few replacement openers had suggested themselves. Smith, we knew, had spent the winter training and practising in England. Then there were a couple of players on the 'A' tour to Zimbabwe. The favourite was Mike Atherton, who had done tremendously well in Zimbabwe and Kenya – and, incidentally, had proved more than useful as a leg-break bowler; but he was now suffering from a groin strain and could not be risked. Then there was young Graham Thorpe, the Surrey left-hander, who had also been a success on the tour. But we felt it would not be fair to bring a youngster with no Test experience and pitch him straight into two vital matches against the full might of the West Indies fast bowlers. So we happily settled for 'Smudge' Smith.

He couldn't be there in time to play against Barbados so, with Alec opening, we were thrown back on our emergency wild card – none other than David Gower. It didn't matter that David had not been picked for the original tour party: we all knew he was still a great batsman, and there was never any doubt in my mind that he would play for England again. But now there was a chance it would be sooner than expected!

It was no problem, for Micky Stewart or me, that David had not been selected for the original party: we were in a bit of a spot and the man who could help us out of it was right there in the press box. We didn't even feel it was necessary to call Lord's – either then or later.

I knew David would be keen to help. Only a week earlier I had said to him, more as a joke than anything else, that we might have to call on him at some time. It was obvious from his reaction that he did not find the idea too distasteful, so we brought him into the game against Barbados, as much as anything else to give us a breather while we sorted out our injuries and David Smith shrugged off his jet lag and had some practice.

As it turned out, we had a spare batting place for the Barbados game, anyway. We wanted to give Jack Russell a rest as he had played throughout the tour and would be facing two Tests, one after the other, as the tour reached its climax. But that gave us a problem with the wicket-keeping position. Alec Stewart had been carrying a damaged finger for most of the tour, and while it was OK for him to field and bat, it would obviously be risky for him behind the stumps.

Robert Bailey, who had done the job a few times for Northants, agreed to help out by keeping against Barbados. But after a couple of hours his hands were bruised and causing him some discomfort, so we called on David Bairstow, who had toured the West Indies with England in 1981 and was now here with Yorkshire on their pre-season trip. We had to have permission from Desmond Haynes, the Barbados captain, and the umpires, but they didn't raise any objections. David was a great help and we were very grateful to him; but Jack Russell's absence gave us an extra batting place. And that was where Gower came in.

After all that had happened to him – not being originally selected and not having batted for six months – David was understandably nervous about playing. It was a relief to me when he finally accepted. He batted only once, going in at number six, and he was just starting to find his touch when he was caught at square leg, which was a little unlucky. The game itself was disappointing as it petered out into a tame draw, with Barbados batting on

in their second innings to a point where we had no chance
of scoring the runs and they had little hope of bowling us
out. But we got in some useful practice – though not as
much as Gordon Greenidge, who made 183 in their first
innings, or Carlisle Best, who scored 95 and 71.

Our two spinners, Eddie Hemmings and Keith Medlycott, bowled quite well, but only Nasser Hussain, who
scored 70 in the first innings, and David Capel, 51 not
out in the second, took advantage of the chance to make
some runs. This game, incidentally, was Allan Lamb's
first as captain of an England team and he took it on
with his customary panache. I think he did a good job
as captain in all the matches he was in charge – the three
in Barbados and the final Test in Antigua. I was in the
dressing room most of the time; but I strongly believe
that the man who is in charge should be calling the shots
and running the team. Obviously, I talked things over
with Allan and Micky Stewart during the match and
during the intervals throughout the match, and said a
few words of encouragement to the lads. But Lambie
had to have their respect as he was the one who led them
on the field; so he took the team talks before they went
out, and while the match was in progress I felt it was only
right for him to take full control.

I must admit it was hard for me as captain of the tour.
I had no wish to interfere with what Lambie wanted to
do, but I wanted to retain some sort of overall influence.
In the end, it was his decision to ask the West Indies to
bat after he won the toss in both the three-day game
against Barbados and in the fourth Test. But we had
all talked about it and we felt that, if there was ever
going to be anything in the Bridgetown pitch to help
the bowlers, it would come on the first day. It was
not a defensive move – we just felt that bowling first

on that pitch would suit our strong points better than batting. The trouble is that you can never be absolutely sure: sometimes things don't work out in quite the way you expect. That's what happened to us, especially in the Test, where the pitch turned out to be a very good one and never gave us the help we had hoped for early on, even though we made the perfect start when Desmond Haynes was out without scoring.

Our first job now after one day's practice was to find a team for the final limited-overs international. If David Gower had made 60 or 70 runs against Barbados, he would have been considered and would very likely have played. But it was felt he would be better off having some practice with his new Hampshire colleagues, who were also in Barbados on a pre-season tour. It was understood that Gower would still be under consideration if we had any further injury problems, and he was happy to fall in with that arrangement.

It was good to have the chance to talk with Mark Nicholas, the Hampshire captain, who had led the England 'A' tour to Zimbabwe and Kenya. Unfortunately, Mark suddenly went down with malaria, which he had presumably caught in Africa, within a few days of arriving in Barbados – but not before he had filled me in on what had happened on his tour. It seems to have been almost a mirror image of ours, with the lads showing a lot of keenness and will to win. Mark said that everyone thought well of the management team of Bob Bennett, of Lancashire, and my old Essex captain Keith Fletcher. It all seemed to be a good portent for the future.

I had to feel sorry for Mark. No sooner had he arrived in Barbados than he was in the Queen Elizabeth Hospital. He spent two days in the public ward, where I visited him a couple of times, before being moved to a

private room. Thankfully he came out after a few days
and made an appearance at the Test ground, though he
was looking a trifle pale and wobbly.

Our immediate problem was to give David Smith
enough practice for him to be ready for the one-day
international and then, hopefully, for the Test. He had
a net on the Sunday, the day he arrived – an occasion
that, disastrously, cost us the services of Gus Fraser
for the rest of the tour. Gus injured his side bowling
to 'Smudge' and found the injury impossible to throw
off the before the end of the tour. That was a real blow
as Gus had been one of our most consistent bowlers,
and none of the West Indian batsmen had ever looked
completely happy against him.

We found a game for Smith with a local club side – the
Wanderers – who were playing against Hampshire, and
he made a 50 in that match, which was very encouraging.
We also tried to fix him up with a game for Yorkshire,
but Steve Oldham, the county coach, said it wouldn't be
possible since they had gone to Barbados to give their
own players as much practice as possible.

It was a pity but, in the end, it didn't make much
difference. Smith is a tall left-hander who plays straight,
and it is well known that he is not one to be intimidated
by fast bowling. He had toured the West Indies in 1986
and did quite well in the three Tests he played, so I had
no fears about putting him in the Test. But there was one
thing we hadn't allowed for: David had batted quite well
for over half an hour in the one-day international when
he suddenly started to have rather a torrid time at the
hands of Ezra Moseley, the bowler who had broken
my finger in Trinidad. He was hit on the helmet and
then took a bang on his bottom hand, in his case the
left one, before being bowled. It soon turned out that

his left thumb had been fractured – so he was out for the rest of the tour!

It was rotten luck for a man who had hoped to seize the chance to pump new life into his Test career. It was also rotten luck for the team as a whole. We had been doing so well up to the third Test in Trinidad. Now the crop of injuries was threatening to undermine all the confidence and spirit we had worked so hard to develop.

Morning rain, plus the West Indies' rather slow rate, reduced the one-day international to 38 overs, so we did very well to reach 214 for three. Wayne Larkins and Allan Lamb played well, but I thought Robin Smith's 69 was one of the best innings I have seen. Robin is, of course, a naturally aggressive batsman; he hits particularly hard square on the offside and is also a very fine puller. What I chiefly remember about this particular knock is the tremendous power of his shots: you'd hear the sound of bat on ball and then, almost immediately, the crack as the ball walloped into the boundary boards. Ned, Lambie and Robin set a tremendous pace and we made our total of 214 in only 38 overs. Of the West Indies' fast bowlers, only Ambrose was reasonably economical; Marshall went for 50 runs in 8 overs, Walsh for 49 in 8, and Moseley for 43 in 7.

But the West Indies batted well too – and we didn't bowl as well as we can, apart from Gladstone Small, who took 3 for 29 in 9 overs. Our line and length, the two qualities we had been working on all the tour, suffered: Phil DeFreitas went for 63 in just over 8 overs, while David Capel conceded 53 in 6. Richie Richardson made a brilliant 80 and Carlisle Best, who revelled in the three matches against us in his native Barbados, also played well for 51. This was his lowest score in a fortnight in which he scored 398 runs in four knocks, before being injured in the Test.

West Indies won with three balls to spare, which was a setback for us. We hadn't played too well in the two previous one-day internationals in Guyana, and I always set out to win every game I'm involved in. As I have said, winning can become a habit and it was a habit I wanted the England team to re-acquire. Yet on this tour, if you include the unofficial international we played in Guyana when the Test was washed out, we had lost all four limited-over matches, which was a disappoinment after having built up such a good one-day record against the West Indies in the past few years.

There was one little incident in that game that nobody seemed to pick on at the time, but it did make quite a big show in the papers a couple of days later. It was the sort of flare-up that can happen in the heat of the moment, but luckily this one was nipped in the bud and was soon forgotten, which is just as well.

Gladstone Small thought he had trapped Gordon Greenidge lbw early in the West Indies innings, but the umpire gave the batsman the benefit of the doubt. When Gladstone had Greenidge caught behind some time later, he shouted something like 'That's the second time I've had you'. Greenidge must have thought Gladstone had sworn at him and he waded angrily into a group of England players before going back to the pavilion. Then, at the presentation after the game, Greenidge grabbed Small by the shirt and seemed to want to continue the argument. They were pulled apart, but the incident had been seen by our manager Peter Lush, who felt obliged to report it to the West Indies Board. They held a full meeting to discuss the incident and issued Greenidge with a severe reprimand. He later apologized and, as far as we were concerned, that was an end to the matter.

By now we had enough problems of our own to worry about, anyway. There didn't seem much hope of David Smith being fit for either this Test in Barbados or the final one in Antigua. And my injury, though it was coming on well, still looked like keeping me out for the rest of the tour. I had made two or three visits to Winston Searle, the orthopaedic surgeon in Barbados who was treating me. He said that I was improving well and that the pins that had been inserted were doing their job. I also made a number of visits to an occupational therapist, a very pleasant English lady named Suzie Marsden. She was very helpful to me and made a sling to keep my left arm up and some straps to hold the little finger of my left hand – the one with the break – firmly against the third finger to prevent it moving about.

She also gave me some orthopaedic putty to squeeze in order to strengthen my finger and help it to move again. Apparently with fractures like mine there are two ways to help the mending process. You can either encase the finger in plaster, with the pins still in. This immobilizes it efficiently; but when the plaster comes off and the pins are taken out, the hand will have become stiff and it can be very hard to regain the movement.

The other method is the one they favoured for me. That is to have a light strap just to keep the two fingers together while you work them around during the healing period. That can be quite painful, and after you've done it for 10 minutes or so, you put a bit of ice on them. The fingers will then stiffen up and feel quite sore for a time. But in the long run it pays dividends, because when the injury finally heals you get full movement back much more quickly.

It was the short run that bothered me, however: I had to face the fact that I was not going to make it for the Barbados Test. With David Smith and Gus Fraser also out, we had to re-jig the side. (We had thought Fraser might make the Test if we didn't risk him in the one-day international two days earlier, but it was not to be.)

Phil DeFreitas came in to replace him and in the end did a reasonable job, taking five wickets in all. We felt that Alec Stewart, who had batted a fair amount of time in the Barbados game, was our best bet to open with Wayne Larkins, Rob Bailey moved up to his more accustomed position of number three, and Nasser Hussain came back after missing the Trinidad Test with his injured wrist. So we had quite a few changes – and that always disrupts the balance. But we had plenty of good players in the squad and it was a chance for them to show what they could do.

It was Allan Lamb's first Test as captain, and the importance of it wasn't lost on him. We were still one up in the series, so even a draw would take us to Antigua with the West Indies still needing to win. It turned out to be a tremendous Test match with some outstanding performances. The result went against us in the end, but we took the game to the last hour and I assured everyone afterwards that they had nothing to be ashamed of.

We won the toss and, as I have already said, we fielded. We took that early wicket, but after that things did not really work out for us. Devon Malcolm failed to match up to his past performances and, to be frank, had a bad game. That is going to happen sometimes. He is still inexperienced: he bowled too short and was cut and pulled and, more to the point, went for a lot of runs. Obviously he was very disappointed, but that's all part of learning to be a top-class bowler.

At the end of the first day the West Indies were 311 for five, with Best 100 not out. We had done quite well to take five wickets, but if we had bowled tighter – and Dev was not the only culprit – we might have restricted them to about 250. With over 300 they were well on the way to a big score. The wicket had not done as much as we expected. Sometimes you put a side in and the wicket simply doesn't behave as as you had predicted. This was one of those days.

On the second day we managed to bowl them out for 446, which wasn't too bad. Best went on to score 164, his maiden Test century. It was a magnificent innings, and he had really come good after struggling somewhat against us in the first two Tests, even though he did make 64 in the second innings in Jamaica.

Best made his debut against us in the 1986 tour, but failed to make a big score. He's not so well known in England as most of his team-mates as he didn't make the 1988 tour. And so we tend to regard him as a new face, although he's 28 years old. He's got all the shots in the book, though he prefers to hit square rather than straight. He's also a fine fielder – especially at slip, where I would say he's as good as anyone in the world at present. Ironically, it was on one of the rare occasions that he put one down in the slips that he broke his finger – which meant that he missed the fifth Test.

Best has (or at least had) the habit of talking to himself while batting. I don't mean the occasional muttering that many batsmen indulge in to gee themselves up between balls. No, Best would deliver a detailed running commentary from the moment the bowler started his run up. It would include delivery of the ball, Best's shot, cover-point's failure to intercept its progress to the boundary, and announcement of the crowd's applause.

I think he must have been an avid listener to radio cricket commentaries in his young days.

The innings that interested me most from my seat on the balcony, though, was the 70 made by Vivian Richards, back in the West Indies team again after missing the Trinidad Test through illness. He seemed to have a tremendous determination about him that was missing in the first Test, where he tried to dominate the bowling and hit everything for four: in Jamaica he had given chances and had never really looked set. In this knock in Barbados he looked more like the old Viv Richards I used to watch and play against 10 years ago. While hitting a fair number of boundaries, he seemed also to be more watchful, more cautious and more solid. In short, he looked like the great player that he is – and that was bad news for England.

He was bitterly disappointed when he came off after being caught by Jack Russell off David Capel's bowling. You could tell that he desperately wanted a hundred, and he sat by himself on the steps leading to the dressing room for almost half an hour and not talking to anyone. I think he felt he had a point to prove, especially to the English press, who were foolishly writing him off as finished. He wanted to prove he wasn't over the hill and still had a lot of good cricket in him – a fact which was obvious to me; but Viv felt he wanted to show the world.

While on the subject of Richards, I have to mention the man who caught him – our wicket-keeper Jack Russell. He was absolutely brilliant behind the stumps in their first innings – truly world-class. There were no byes in their total of 446 and he took five catches in the innings. He was absolutely immaculate. He has really come on, and to me and many other England players he looks

Nasser Hussain, batting with a broken wrist, avoids further injury by pulling out of the way of a Courtney Walsh bouncer during his knock off 35 in the first innings of the fifth Test in Antigua.

This one had nothing to do with me. Viv Richards lays down the law
in the Press Box on the Saturday of the Antigua Test.

Robin Smith is hit by Courtney
Walsh in Antigua.

Joy for Ian Bishop – that's another
of his eight wickets in Antigua.

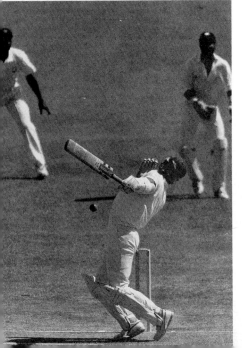

Gordon Greenidge may be reaching the veteran stage, but he was still one of the West Indies best batsmen against us, scoring 308 runs at an average of 44.

Done it! Desmond Haynes celebrates his 100 in Antigua.

The board tells it all – the West Indies have passed us without losing a wicket.

BATSMEN

NO 1 RUNS 130 NO 2 RUNS 116

EXTRAS 14

SCORE

RUNS   WKTS

260

OVERS 62

REMAINING 79

INNINGS TOTALS

ENGLAND   1ST. 260

1ST.

Back home again – and I start the English season with a century against Middlesex at Lord's. Let's hope I can keep it up for the rest of the season.

the best keeper in the world. He is a tremendous little cricketer and a fighter.

I thought we batted fairly well after an early setback when Wayne Larkins was caught off the second ball of the innings – not really the ideal start. Alec Stewart gave a reasonable account of himself as an opener, Allan Lamb made another tremendous hundred and Robin Smith gave him good support. We made a decent total of 358, but I thought we were a bit unlucky during the last session on the third day. Jack Russell and Nasser Hussain were going well and looked like batting out the day when they were both given out lbw, Jack to Bishop and Nasser to Marshall. That can happen, of course, and I don't really know what the decisions were like, but one, at least, did look a bit suspect. That's neither here nor there now, but it did prevent us from batting out the third day – even though Phil DeFreitas made a useful 24 – and probably kept us from a score nearer 400. It also stopped us from killing a bit more time at the end of the day.

But 350-odd was still a reasonable score, and at that stage it was a fair contest. I was still very hopeful of achieving at least the draw we wanted. So it became quite a battle when the West Indies went in to bat again. We tried to slow things down as much as we could and they were obviously intent on making their runs as fast as they could, running the singles and taking everything that was going. They were very positive, with Haynes contributing a solid, forceful century, and were able to declare over 350 ahead, leaving us an hour to bat before the end of the fourth day.

Only an hour! But it was in those 60 minutes – more than in any other period on the tour – that we lost the series. We lost three wickets in that last session – including the night watchman, Small – and at 15 for three overnight, we had a lot to do on the final day to save the game.

It was unlikely we were going to score the 345 we needed on the last day to win, and on the few occasions when we hinted that we might have a go at it, the West Indies would slow the over rate down. Not that we could point the finger at them on that score: we had done exactly the same thing when they began to accelerate in their second innings. After all, the earlier they declared, the longer would we have to bat in the final innings to save the match.

But those three wickets we lost on the fourth evening were important, and one of them, at least, caused a certain amount of controversy. There was a lot of press comment and a subsequent row between Christopher Martin-Jenkins, of the BBC, and a lot of local people over the comments he made on air. The dismissal in question was that of Rob Bailey, caught down the leg side by Jeffrey Dujon off the bowling of Curtly Ambrose. It was a crucial wicket as it exposed the night watchman, Gladstone Small, who was also soon out lbw to Ambrose. I must say it looked from the pavilion as if the ball had come off Bailey's thigh pad as it went through to Dujon. The row erupted when it seemed to be implied that the umpire, Lloyd Barker, had been pressurized into giving Bailey out by the way the West Indies appealed and by the way their emotions got the better of them. But cricketers *do* get excited on the big occasion, and the the West Indians obviously thought Rob had hit it. You simply must accept the umpire's decision. Without umpires you wouldn't be able to play the game.

It's disappointing when you think a decision is not right – especially when you are involved, as we were, in an absolutely crucial match on an overseas tour. But you have to take the rough with the smooth. If you get uptight about these things, the only thing to suffer will be your own game.

The first of those three wickets, sadly, was that of Wayne Larkins, caught behind for his second nought of the game. I know how he felt – bagging a pair in a Test match is not the most uplifting experience in the world. And we were desperately in need of Ned's experience and solidity in the situation we had landed ourselves in. He had been playing well for most of the tour, and he was desperately disappointed that he hadn't contributed much in this game. But that's the way cricket goes; it can be very cruel at times.

I was pleased with the way the lads never gave up the fight on the last day. We lost Alec Stewart in the first session and Allan Lamb in the second, and several more went in quick succession to the new ball after Richards had bowled 10 overs of his off-spin to hasten departure of the old. But there was still less than an hour and 11.2 overs left when Devon Malcolm became the last wicket to fall. We had lost by 164 runs, the West Indies had squared the series, and Ambrose had bowled as well as I have seen him to take eight for 45. He is becoming a truly formidable talent and will, I think, soon take on the mantle of the great Joel Garner. More to the point, with Marshall reaching the veteran stage, Bishop and Ambrose are both coming to their peak at a crucial time.

A word about over rates. Over the past decade or so – in fact, ever since they based their attack on four genuinely fast bowlers – the West Indies have been criticized for their slow over rates. I think the criticism has often been justified. It was certainly justified in the

1990 tour; but it has to be admitted that England's rate was little, if any, better. In each England innings in the fourth Test, Viv Richards put himself on for a longish spell in order to speed up the business of getting through the required number of overs to take the new ball. Bowling his off-spin to very defensive fields, Richards conceded only 14 runs in 9 overs in the first innings and 11 in 10 in the second.

It's fair to say that neither side looked remotely like getting through the requirement of 90 overs per day during this Test series. Apart from the four drinks breaks – one in the morning, two in the afternoon and one after tea – the great heat, which discourages undue haste, and the various kinds of time-wasting indulged in by both sides, it has to be remembered that the series was played in the spring, when the tropical evening begins early and abruptly. Close-of-play was officially at five past five, but play invariably ended later, at about 5.40, because of the slow over rate – and by that time it was getting quite murky. But still, when all's said and done, it should be perfectly possible to bowl 15 overs an hour even with an attack consisting entirely of pace bowlers. In the West Indies (as quite often elsewhere) the average in the Tests was no more than 13; and on one occasion the West Indies bowled only eight in the course of an hour's play.

All was now set for the final showdown in Antigua. There was only one day between the Test in Barbados and the one in Antigua – not the ideal preparation, especially as we had so many injuries we were trying to clear up. I know the programme had to be squeezed in to allow us to return home in time for the start of the English season, but our lads were becoming pretty exhausted by this time, and I really don't think they should have been asked to play two Tests back-to-back at the end of such an arduous tour.

Allan Lamb and I had managed to grab one day's relaxation when a chap called Professor Edwards, who used to play for Barbados, took us out in his boat for a few hours' fishing. We left at about six in the morning and cruised around in the area off Sam Lord's Castle, where we caught four biggish fish. One of them, a dolphin fish, or dorado, you regularly see on the menu in local fish restaurants; it's not a genuine dolphin, of course – it just looks a bit like a small version of one. Our biggest catch was a kingfish, locally known as a wahoo. This one scaled about 28 pounds and took quite a bit of landing. It wasn't easy for me with my broken hand, but we parked the rods in the cleats on the side of the boat and all we had to do was to reel the fish in.

Long before the Barbados Test was over the island was almost sinking under the weight of English fans who had come out to enjoy the cricket and the sunshine. There must have been all of 3,000 of them in the Bridgetown Oval – as well as almost all the players' wives and girl-friends. As I've said before, I don't mind the wives and families being with us, but it must have some effect on the team spirit as the players must, inevitably, go their own way more in the evenings when their wives are with them and we don't get together quite as much as we would normally. That was especially true in a hotel like the Rockley Resort, where we were staying in Barbados. We were all in separate apartments spread out over quite a large area, and even at the best of times we never saw much of each other. That can be a disadvantage, but nothing that can't be overcome as long as everyone is sensible and keeps in mind the real reason we are there – to play cricket.

At this point I have to confess to unwitting complicity in the mysterious disappearance of Rob Bailey's overnight bag. My wife Brenda had arrived for a holiday in Antigua with our three daughters, Hannah and the twins Megan and Sally. As might be expected, they're a bit of a handful at the best of times, so Brenda had brought Karen Kaye, the girlfriend of Essex batsman Alan Lilley, to give her a bit of a hand.

Now it so happened that, somewhere on the journey from Barbados to Antigua, Rob's bag went missing. It was not particularly serious – it contained only his casual clothes and leisure wear. But he was having to borrow from the other lads and it was a bit awkward. British Airways asked in London to see if the bag had stayed on the aircraft and ended up at Heathrow, but no luck.

I told Rob not to worry. I thought it would turn up sooner or later – probably in the room of one of the players; perhaps one of their wives had picked it up by mistake. But almost as soon as I had shared these comforting thoughts with Rob, I noticed an unopened bag in Karen's room. I didn't think anything further of it until a couple of days later, when I happened to ask if it was hers – it had no labels or means of identification on it.

When she said she hadn't seen it before in her life, it seemed worth taking a closer look . . . a look which revealed a label bearing the name 'Robert Bailey.' My only problem now was to explain to him that all the time he had been going around in borrowed gear his own stuff was gathering dust in the room of the lady who was helping to look after my children.

And so we prepared ourselves to play the final Test of a series that had seen English cricket climb back off the floor in a way few people had thought possible when we flew out of Gatwick less than three months before. We still needed no more than a draw to end the series all square – something that would have been very acceptable to us all before we left England.

We still had plenty of problems. David Smith had a cracked thumb and, although we didn't know it, Nasser Hussain's painful wrist was, in fact, broken. It hadn't shown up when he was X-rayed in Guyana a month earlier and he had continued to play. This was a pity because, if we had known the extent of the injury at the time, we would have sent him home and asked for a replacement. The faulty diagnosis didn't help us – and it would mean Nasser's services would also be lost to Essex for the first few weeks of the 1990 season.

Nasser had carried on, and for a while the injury seemed to be improving. But during the Antigua Test the pain became worse and we sent him for another X-ray, which confirmed that it was broken. Obviously we didn't want the West Indies to know, so we had to keep it secret. But the very fact of Nasser's injury underlined our need to have an adequate replacement standing by. And that was where David Gower came in again.

Even with Nasser we had only seven batsmen – the minimum, in my view – and no cover. I firmly believe in having a balanced team, which means seven batsmen, one of whom – in this case David Capel – is the all-rounder. The question of whether all your bowlers are fast or you include a spinner doesn't come into it. The important thing is to make enough runs to allow you to dictate the course of the game.

If you make a decent score, you are always in the game; if you make a really big one, you force your opponents to start thinking about saving the game rather than winning it. That's why Capel played in all the games at number seven because he is a genuine batsman as well as a bowler and gave us a better balanced side. If you replace your all-rounder with a specialist bowler, your batting begins to look a bit thin. We had to take into consideration the fact that, however well they had done, many of our specialist batsmen were inexperienced, at least at Test match level. And now, with Gus Fraser missing the last two Tests, we crucially lost some of our balance in the bowling department. He and Gladstone Small had been two bowling bankers: the two guys we could rely on to plug away, with testing line and length, for over after over.

I'm not trying to use injuries as an excuse for the things that went wrong at the end of the tour. They're all part of the game – and the West Indies had their problems, too, with Malcolm Marshall, Ezra Moseley and Carlisle Best ruled out of the Antigua Test. But it's obviously easier for the home team in those circumstances as they have more players they can call on. Gus was important to us and we gave him every chance to make it for the final Test. He had a workout the day before the game and, although his side was still a bit sore, it wasn't any worse. So we gave him another try-out on the morning of the match. We would have liked to include him, but he still wasn't right; and even if we had known we were going to win the toss and bat, it wouldn't have made any difference. The way Gus was, even another day would not have been enough for him to recover sufficiently for us to risk playing him.

Another problem was that David Smith had been in the nets a couple of times and was clearly struggling. Allan Lamb had watched him and had seen that he was in pain almost every time he played the ball. So we were down to the bare bones of our batting. With this in mind we once again asked David Gower to stand by and he had agreed to fly with us from Barbados to Antigua and join the 13 for the final Test. He had never been led to believe that he would definitely play, so it was misguided of people to suggest that he had been badly treated when, finally, he was left out. I am sure he was disappointed – I would have expected him to be. Any cricketer would be excited about playing in a Test match and David was no exception, especially after all he had been through.

But I stress that David knew he was never more than a stand-by. He was there in case one of the batsmen was taken ill or fell downstairs the night before the game. We were very grateful to him for standing by, but when everyone reported fit he was released, and he flew home to England on the rest day (the day after the Test started).

While we are on the subject of players being sent home when they are badly injured, perhaps I should explain why I decided to stay after I broke my hand in Trinidad. I can honestly say that the question of returning early to England never arose. There were only two Tests to play, and I wanted to stay to retain a sense of continuity in our party. We were in a good position after the draw in Trinidad and I wanted to give moral support to the boys. Allan Lamb was responsible for motivating the team in the dressing room and on the field once the game was in progress. But before the game I would say a few words at the team meeting – as would Lambie and Micky Stewart. I also continued to help pick the sides, and it was still my job to have a word with the guys who had been left out.

I naturally took more of a back seat once the game started and – although the problem never arose – I would have had to let Allan have his way if there had been any disagreement about the make-up of the team – just as I would have had my way when I was captain.

Micky Stewart, of course, also gave us his views and advice, but to be honest there was never any disagreement between us three. The fourth member at these meetings would be Peter Lush, but although he contributed to discussions on various tour matters, he didn't say anything about the players, and he took no part in team-selection meetings. Finally, of course, there was our physio, Laurie Brown, who kept us up to date on fitness and injuries and told us whether a player was going to make it through a five-day Test match. But in the end it was up to three of us – Lambie, Micky and me – to decide the make-up of our best side.

So that was it: try as we might to have Fraser and Smith fit, we had not been lucky and we went into the final Test with the same team that had lost in Barbados when the West Indies levelled the series.

We won the toss and batted because it looked a good wicket and there didn't seem any reason to Lambie or me why we should field first. One writer suggested we were deluding ourselves if we thought we could beat the West Indies by batting first. He said we should have considered sticking them in so that we would not have to face their bowlers from the start. It just shows how little conception that guy has of how the game is played at Test match level.

We batted first because it looked like a good wicket – the best one we had played on in the series – but we thought it might deteriorate as the match went on; there was simply no good reason to bowl first on it. As it turned out, the wicket stayed pretty much the same throughout; in fact Micky went so far as to say it was the best pitch he had ever seen. It didn't seam around much, but it favoured the taller fast bowlers because, if you banged it in, you did manage to get some bounce out of it.

Andy Roberts, who had helped prepare the wicket, said that if you really put something into it, you would get something out, which was fair enough. But, really, it was a tremendous batting wicket. And that made it all the more disappointing when we were out for only 260 in the first innings.

That's where we lost the match. On any wicket you need to bat well at least once. If you bat badly in your first innings, you are under pressure. On a pitch as good as the one at St John's you can't afford to bat badly even once. Our total of 260 was doubly disheartening when you consider that we had 143 on the board before we lost our third wicket.

That's not to say the West Indies didn't bowl well. Bishop, who is a terrific prospect at only 22 years of age, took five for 84 in 28 overs, and Courtney Walsh, coming on first change, gave away only 51 runs in 21 overs, picking up three wickets. Nonetheless, the quality of the wicket as a batting strip meant that, batting first, we couldn't be satisfied with less than 350 and that we could feel comfortable only with something like 400.

The next day was Good Friday, the rest day, and when the match resumed on the Saturday we had our worst day of the whole series. Our bowlers seemed thoroughly exhausted after the rest day. Gladstone Small, who had been one of the great successes of the tour, looked tired, and so did David Capel. They started off as if they had already bowled 80 overs; I suppose that all the effort they had put in over the previous two and a half months was finally catching up with them. Whatever the reason, Greenidge and Haynes showed us how it should be done: their opening partnership of 298 equalled their own Test record and put the West Indies well along the road to victory in the match and the series. As a pair, these two have been the best openers of the past decade and among the best since the war. It may not be quite as exhilarating a partnership as its predecessor, Greenidge and Fredericks, but Haynes has proved to be a rock-solid and prolific opener in both Tests and one-day internationals.

Greenidge, incidentally, was run out for the second time in the series – and just as unnecessarily as the first time. After he went, the West Indies lost their other nine wickets for only 145 runs – but still, that meant a total of 446, a first-innings lead of 186. Dev Malcolm picked up four wickets and, interestingly, was more economical than either Small or Capel.

We had flown out of Bridgetown the night of the last day of the Barbados Test and we hadn't arrived at our Antigua hotel until well after midnight. We tried to practise the next day as it was the only chance we would have before the Test, but in the end it was all too much for us. You could say it was the same for the West Indies, but they had two fresh bowlers in Courtney Walsh and Eldine Baptiste who hadn't played in Barbados, and at that stage of the series it made a difference.

I'm not criticizing our bowlers. It was a flat wicket and it needed a lot of effort to get anything at all out of it. They just didn't seem to have it in them any more.

Even so, they fought back well on the third day when they took 10 wickets for about 150 runs. But in the context of the game the West Indies were still in the driving seat as we were left with two days to bat to save it. But it was a good fight-back and it is well worth mentioning.

The really sad thing was that we lost Wayne Larkins in the gloom right at the end of the third day, and no sooner was he out than they came off for bad light. I know how he felt – the same thing happened to me in the famous Test match against the Aussies at Leeds in 1981. I was caught Alderman, bowled Lillee and when Mike Brearley came in at number three he faced two balls before the umpires called it off for the light. It's not the first time it's happened and it won't be the last. But it's still very annoying all the same.

I can remember John Emburey being bowled by a full toss from Colin Croft at St John's in 1981 by a ball he backed away from because he never saw it. It might have been going straight at his head for all he knew. Larkins was out at the same end. The ball sometimes comes down in line with the edge of the screen and out of the faces of the members in the pavilion and it can be very difficult to pick up.

The main disappointment to me was that we didn't play well. In the other three Tests we had played some tremendous cricket, even in the one at Barbados which we lost. That was a hard-fought match and even though they won, it went to the last hour and we were in the game all the way. In this one they were on top all through and, frankly, gave us a hiding. That was disappointing because we had set out to improve our cricket and really stand up to the West Indies. When they beat us 5–0, 5–0 and 4–0, we just didn't compete: they simply rolled us over in every game. But this time they knew they had been in a game of cricket.

I think that at the beginning they thought that, while we weren't going to be a pushover, they were very confident that they were going to win. But after losing the first match and very nearly the second as well, they had to think twice about what they were going to do.

They did their homework, they applied themselves admirably, and in the end you had to give them credit for the way they fought back. Needless to say, when the West Indies finally won the series that we had dominated for so long our lads were very deflated. But for most of the tour they had done all the right things and had achieved everything they set out to do. Our performances were good, our attitude was good and loads of good things came out of the tour. The determination to win was apparent to all. They played like people who were proud to represent their country. And I was proud to lead them on tour.

Scorecards

ENGLAND XI V BARBADOS XI

at Kensington Oval, Bridgetown, Barbados
30 January, 1990

England XI

G.A. Gooch (capt)	c and b Johnson	3
R.J. Bailey	c Alleyne, b Maxwell	11
R.A. Smith	c Puckerin, b Springer	27
N. Hussain	c Alleyne, b Johnson	78
D.J. Capel	run out	43
A.J. Stewart	c Springer, b Maxwell	21
*R.C. Russell	not out	16
P.A.J. DeFreitas	not out	14
E.E. Hemmings		
A.R.C. Fraser		
D.E. Malcolm		
	lb 3, w 7, nb 14	24
	TOTAL for 6 wickets (50 overs)	237

	O	M	R	W
Johnson	10	2	43	2
Maxwell	9	1	37	2
Springer	10	1	38	1
Roach	10	1	48	–
Matthews	6	–	36	–
Alleyne	5	–	32	–

Fall of wickets
1–23, 2–23, 3–78, 4–180, 5–204, 6–213

Barbados XI

M.H.W. Inniss	c Gooch, b Fraser	38
P. Wallace	b Capel	49
S. Campbell	lbw, b Hemmings	29
M.L. Sealy	b DeFreitas	4
P.J.C. Alleyne (capt)	b DeFreitas	4
M. Matthews	c Russell, b DeFreitas	2
*L.K. Puckerin	c DeFreitas, b Malcolm	14
T. Roach	b DeFreitas	1
D. Springer	c Hussain, b Malcolm	2
A.L Johnson	not out	38
G. Maxwell	lbw, b Fraser	13
	lb 8, w 6, nb 9	23
	TOTAL (46.3 overs)	217

	O	M	R	W
Malcolm	10	–	47	2
Fraser	9.3	2	21	2
DeFreitas	10	–	59	4
Capel	6	–	47	1
Hemmings	10	3	33	1
Gooch	1	–	2	–

Fall of wickets
1–83, 2–125, 3–131, 4–131, 5–135, 6–141, 7–146, 8–159, 9–160
Umpires – S. Parris & N. Harrison
Toss – England XI

England XI won by 20 runs

ENGLAND XI V LEEWARD ISLANDS

at Warner Park, Basseterre, St Kitts
2, 3, 4 and 5 February, 1990

England XI	first innings		second innings	
G.A. Gooch (capt)	c Harris, b W. Benjamin	46	c and b Guishard	50
W. Larkins	c and b Arthurton	107	b Guishard	27
A.J. Stewart	c sub, b Guishard	125	(6) c sub, b Guishard	28
R.A. Smith	b Guishard	71	(5) b Anthony	37
N. Hussain	b Guishard	42	(4) lbw, b Arthurton	10
R.J. Bailey	lbw, b Anthony	1	(3) c sub, b Arthurton	10
*R.C. Russell	not out	15	not out	32
P.A.J. DeFreitas	not out	17	not out	6
K.T. Medlycott				
G.C. Small				
D.E. Malcolm				
	B 2, lb 9, w 5, nb 4	20	B 5, lb 7, w 1	13
	TOTAL for 6 wks., dec.	444	TOTAL for 6 wks., dec.	213

	O	M	R	W	O	M	R	W
K.C.G. Benjamin	6	4	4	–				
W.K.M. Benjamin	21	3	62	1				
Anthony	32	11	79	1	21	3	64	1
Baptiste	32	9	76	–	6	1	14	–
Guishard	53	11	150	3	29.3	8	71	3
Arthurton	11	3	23	1	16	3	31	2
Otto	10	–	39	–				
Richardson					8	3	21	–

Fall of wickets
1–96, 2–220, 3–364, 4–379, 5–380, 6–424;
1–68, 2–91, 3–101, 4–108, 5–156, 6–200

Leeward Islands	first innings		second innings	
R. Bassue	lbw, b Small	21	(2) c Bailey, b Medlycott	57
S.C. Williams	b Small	1	(1) lbw, b Small	31
R.B. Richardson (capt)	c and b Small	83	c Russell, b Malcolm	5
K.L.T. Arthurton	lbw, b DeFreitas	7	b Medlycott	86
R.M. Otto	lbw, b Malcolm	18	not out	51
H. Anthony	b Malcolm	0	c Gooch, b Small	4
*L.L. Harris	c Malcolm, b DeFreitas	19	not out	54
E.A.E. Baptiste	b Malcolm	61		
N.C. Guishard	c Russell, b Small	21		
W.K.M. Benjamin	not out	0		
K.C.G. Benjamin	absent injured	–		
	b 3, lb 8, w 3, nb 11	25	B 4, lb 4, w 1, nb 4	13
	TOTAL	256	TOTAL for 5 wickets	301

	O	M	R	W	O	M	R	W
Malcolm	23	4	86	3	13	1	81	1
Small	23	4	75	4	17	3	64	2
DeFreitas	14	5	53	2	7	1	49	–
Medlycott	5	–	31	–	17	1	99	2

Fall of wickets
1–2, 2–60, 3–72, 4–138, 5–138, 6–146, 7–172, 8–248, 9–256;
1–50, 2–75, 3–140, 4–196, 5–208
Umpires – C. Mack & A.E. Weekes
Toss – England

Match Drawn

ENGLAND XI V WINDWARD ISLANDS

at Mindoo Phillip Park, Castries, St Lucia
8, 9, 10 and 11 February, 1990

Windward Islands	first innings		second innings	
L.D. John	b DeFreitas	83	lbw, b DeFreitas	6
D.T. Telemaque	lbw, b Fraser	20	c Stewart, b Medlycott	43
D.A. Joseph	st Russell, b Medlycott	59	b Hemmings	19
J. Eugene	c Smith, b Fraser	8	c Smith, b Medlycott	17
J.D. Charles (capt)	c Russell, b Capel	39	b Hemmings	10
M. Durand	run out	6	b Medlycott	17
D.J. Collymore	c Lamb, b Hemmings	29	c Gooch	
			b Hemmings	3
*J.R. Murray	c Gooch, b DeFreitas	1	c Gooch, b Medlycott	8
T.Z. Kentish	lbw, b DeFreitas	9	not out	4
W.L. Thomas	st Russell, b Hemmings	19	b Hemmings	1
I.A.B. Allen	not out	0	not out	4
	B 1, lb 4, w 4, nb 35	44	B 4, nb 3	7

	TOTAL			317	TOTAL for 9 wickets			139
	O	M	R	W	O	M	R	W
DeFreitas	22	2	87	3	5	1	25	1
Fraser	22	3	71	2	8	2	33	–
Hemmings	17.3	4	64	2	17	5	41	4
Capel	18	4	46	1				
Medlycott	13	3	44	1	12.2	–	36	4

Fall of wickets
1–73, 2–138, 3–154, 4–228, 5–241, 6–264, 7–270, 8–287, 9–317;
1–12, 2–55, 3–82, 4–101, 5–101, 6–113, 7–126, 8–131, 9–132

England XI	first innings		second innings	
G.A. Gooch	lbw, b Allen	19	c Telemaque, b Collymore	7
W. Larkins	c Murray, b Durand	31	lbw, b Allen	0
A.J. Stewart	lbw, b Collymore	6	b Kentish	77
A.J. Lamb	b Durand	20	c Telemaque, b Kentish	83
R.A. Smith	b Durand	12	c Joseph, b Kentish	19
D.J. Capel	c Telemaque, b Kentish	6	c Telemaque, b Allen	65
*R.C. Russell	b Durand	7	(8) not out	22
P.A.J. DeFreitas	not out	3	(9) c Murray, b Thomas	2
K.T. Medlycott	c Collymore, b Durand	3	(7) run out	21
E.E. Hemmings	c Charles, b Durand	6	lbw, b Allen	1
A.R.C. Fraser	c Charles, b Durand	0	lbw, b Thomas	1
	lb 1, nb 12	13	B 7, lb 3, w 1, nb 17	28
	TOTAL	126	TOTAL	326

	O	M	R	W	O	M	R	W
Allen	9	3	23	1	20	2	55	3
Collymore	11	1	35	1	19	–	59	1
Thomas	7	–	19	–	9.2	1	23	2
Kentish	24	8	33	1	33	6	92	3
Durand	19.4	11	15	7	31	9	55	–
Charles					7	–	32	–

Fall of wickets
1–36, 2–43, 3-87, 4–88, 5–103, 6–111, 7–113, 8–118, 9–124;
1–3, 2–14, 3–166, 4–193, 5–208, 6–272, 7–308, 8–318, 9–325
Umpires – M. Hippolyte & L. Thomas   Toss – Windward Islands

Windward Islands won by one wicket

133

First One-Day International
WEST INDIES V ENGLAND
at Queen's Park Oval, Port of Spain
14 February, 1990

West Indies

C.G. Greenidge	c Stewart, b Capel	21
D.L. Haynes	c Russell, b Lewis	25
R.B. Richardson	c Stewart, b Fraser	51
C.L. Hooper	c Smith, b Hemmings	17
C.A. Best	c and b Gooch	6
I.V.A. Richards (capt)	b Small	32
E.A. Moseley	c Lewis, b Fraser	2
M.D. Marshall	b Small	9
*P.J.L. Dujon	not out	15
I.R. Bishop	not out	18
C.A. Walsh		
	B 4, lb 4, w 3, nb 1	12
	TOTAL for 8 wickets (50 overs)	208

	O	M	R	W
Small	10	1	41	2
Fraser	10	1	37	2
Capel	6	–	25	1
Lewis	7	1	30	1
Hemmings	9	–	41	1
Gooch	8	–	26	1

Fall of wickets
1–49, 2–49, 3–89, 4–100, 5–155, 6–162, 7–172, 8–180

England

G.A. Gooch (capt)	not out	13
W. Larkins	c Best, b Marshall	2
R.A. Smith	not out	6
A.J. Lamb		
A.J. Stewart		
D.J. Capel		
*R.C. Russell		
C.C. Lewis		
E.E. Hemmings		
G.C. Small		
A.R.C. Fraser		
	lb 1, nb 4	5
	TOTAL for 1 wicket (13 overs)	26

	O	M	R	W
Marshall	6	1	12	1
Bishop	5	2	6	–
Walsh	1	–	1	–
Moseley	1	–	6	–

Fall of wicket
1–9
Umpires – C. Cumberbatch & D.A. Archer

Match Abandoned

Second One-Day International
WEST INDIES V ENGLAND
at Queen's Park Oval, Port of Spain, Trinidad
17 February, 1990

West Indies

C.G. Greenidge	not out	8
D.L. Haynes	not out	4
R.B. Richardson		
C.L. Hooper		
C.A. Best		
I.V.A. Richards (capt)		
*P.J.L. Dujon		
E.A. Moseley		
M.D. Marshall		
I.R. Bishop		
C.A. Walsh		
	lb 1	1
TOTAL for no wicket (5.5 overs)		13

	O	M	R	W
Small	3	1	7	–
Fraser	2.5	–	5	–

England
G.A. Gooch (capt)
W. Larkins
R.A. Smith
A.J. Lamb
A.J. Stewart
D.J. Capel
*R.C. Russell
C.C. Lewis
G.C. Small
E.E. Hemmings
A.R.C. Fraser

Umpires – C. Cumberbatch & D.A. Archer

Match Abandoned

ENGLAND XI V JAMAICA
at Sabina Park, Kingston, Jamaica
19, 20 and 21 February, 1990

England XI	first innings		second innings	
G.A. Gooch (capt)	c Staple, b Perry	239		
W. Larkins	c Kennedy, b Haynes	45	retired hurt	124
A.J. Stewart	b Haynes	2	(1) lbw, b Perry	39
A.J. Lamb	c Morgan, b Haynes	31	(3) b Banton	17
R.A. Smith	b Morgan	23	(4) b Banton	0
N. Hussain	run out	14	(5) b Banton	24
D.J. Capel	c Kennedy, b Perry	26	(6) not out	12
*R.C. Russell	c Adams, b Morgan	3	(7) not out	10
A.R.C. Fraser	lbw, b Morgan	3		
E.E. Hemmings	not out	2		
D.E. Malcolm	b Morgan	0		
	B7, lb 2, w 1, nb 7	17	B 9, lb 4, nb 9	22
	TOTAL	405	TOTAL for 4 wks., dec.	248

	O	M	R	W	O	M	R	W
Banton	6	1	25	–	18	3	64	3
Williams	15	3	70	–	14	5	25	–
Davidson	4	–	17	–				
Haynes	43	10	118	3				
Perry	19	2	70	2	18	1	93	1
Carter	10	–	65	–	13	–	53	–
Morgan	17	6	31	4				

Fall of wickets
1–145, 2–149, 3–244, 4–341, 5–363, 6–381, 7–383, 8–403, 9–405;
1–137, 2–180, 3–203, 4–225

Jamaica	first innings		second innings	
D.S. Morgan (capt)	c Russell, b Fraser	10		
R.G. Samuels	b Capel	41	(1) c Smith, b Fraser	5
N. Kennedy	c Russell, b Capel	22		
R. Staple	c Capel, b Malcolm	6	(2) c Hemmings, b Malcolm	25
C.A. Davidson	c Hussain, b Fraser	14		
*J.C. Adams	run out	27	(3) not out	10
R.C. Haynes	c Fraser, b Gooch	98		
L. Williams	b Hemmings	36	(4) not out	0
N.A. Perry	c and b Fraser	35		
C.D. Carter	b Malcolm	12		
C. Banton	not out	0		
	lb 5, w 2, nb 3	10	lb 4	4
	TOTAL	311	TOTAL for 2 wickets	44

	O	M	R	W	O	M	R	W
Malcolm	24	3	88	2	7	1	27	1
Fraser	14.1	1	75	3	7	3	13	1
Capel	22	1	97	2				
Hemmings	16	2	40	1				
Gooch	3	–	6	1				

Fall of wickets
1–17, 2–62, 3–81, 4–88, 5–117, 6–128, 7–217, 8–285, 9–311;
1–12, 2–44
Umpires – L. Bell & A. Gaynor
Toss – England

Match Drawn

139

First Test Match
WEST INDIES V ENGLAND
at Sabina Park, Kingston, Jamaica
24, 25, 26, 28 February and 1 March, 1990

West Indies	first innings		second innings	
C.G. Greenidge	run out	32	c Hussain, b Malcolm	36
D.L. Haynes	c and b Small	36	b Malcolm	14
R.B. Richardson	c Small, b Capel	10	1bw, b Fraser	25
C.A. Best	c Russell, b Capel	4	c Gooch, b Small	64
C.L. Hooper	c Capel, b Fraser	20	c Larkins, b Small	8
I.V.A. Richards (capt)	1bw, b Malcolm	21	b Malcolm	37
*P.J.L. Dujon	not out	19	b Malcolm	15
M.D. Marshall	b Fraser	0	not out	8
I.R. Bishop	c Larkins, b Fraser	0	c Larkins, b Small	3
C.A. Walsh	b Fraser	6	b Small	2
B.P. Patterson	b Fraser	0	run out	2
	B 9, lb 3, nb 4	16	B 14, lb 10, w 1, nb 1	26
	TOTAL	164	TOTAL	240

	O	M	R	W	O	M	R	W
Small	15	6	44	1	22	6	58	4
Malcolm	16	4	49	1	21.3	2	77	4
Fraser	20	8	28	5	14	5	31	1
Capel	13	4	31	2	15	1	50	–

Fall of wickets
1–62, 2–82, 3–92, 4–92, 5–124, 6–144, 7–144, 8–150, 9–164,
1–26, 2–69, 3–87, 4–112, 5–192, 6–222, 7–222, 8–227, 9–237

England	first innings		second innings	
G.A. Gooch (capt)	c Dujon, b Patterson	18	c Greenidge, b Bishop	8
W. Larkins	lbw, b Walsh	46	not out	29
A.J. Stewart	c Best, b Bishop	13	not out	0
A.J. Lamb	c Hooper, b Walsh	132		
R.A. Smith	c Best, b Bishop	57		
N. Hussain	c Dujon, b Bishop	13		
D.J. Capel	c Richardson, b Walsh	5		
*R.C. Russell	c Patterson, b Walsh	26		
G.C. Small	lbw, b Marshall	4		
A.R.C. Fraser	not out	2		
D.E. Malcolm	lbw, b Walsh	0		
	B 23, lb 12, w 1, nb 12	48	lb 1, nb 3	4
	Total	364	Total for one wicket	41

	O	M	R	W	O	M	R	W
Patterson	18	2	74	1	3	1	11	–
Bishop	25	5	72	3	7.3	2	17	1
Marshall	18	3	46	1				
Walsh	27.2	4	68	5	6	–	12	–
Hooper	9	1	28	–				
Richards	9	1	22	–				
Best	4	–	19	–				

Fall of wickets
1–40, 2–60, 3–116, 4–288, 5–315, 6–315, 7–325, 8–339, 9–364,
1–35
Umpires – L.H. Barker & S. Bucknor
Toss – West Indies

England won by 9 wickets

Third One-Day International
WEST INDIES V ENGLAND
at Sabina Park, Kingston, Jamaica
3 March, 1990

England

G.A. Gooch (capt)	b Bishop	2
W. Larkins	b Walsh	33
R.A. Smith	c Marshall, b Hooper	43
A.J. Lamb	b Bishop	66
A.J. Stewart	c Dujon, b Hooper	0
D.J. Capel	c Dujon, b Bishop	28
*R.C. Russell	b Marshall	2
P.A.J. DeFreitas	not out	3
G.C. Small	b Bishop	0
E.E. Hemmings		
A.R.C. Fraser		
	B 4, lb 24, w 6, nb 3	37
	TOTAL for 8 wickets (50 overs)	214

	O	M	R	W
Marshall	10	1	39	1
Bishop	10	1	28	4
Walsh	6	–	38	1
Moseley	6	1	15	–
Richards	9	–	32	–
Hooper	9	–	34	2

Fall of wickets
1–20, 2–71, 3–117, 4–117, 5–185, 6–206, 7–212, 8–214

West Indies

D.L. Haynes	c Smith, b DeFreitas	8
C.A. Best	b Small	4
R.B. Richardson	not out	108
C.L. Hooper	b Hemmings	20
I.V.A. Richards (capt)	c Small, b Hemmings	25
K.L.T. Arthurton	c Russell, b Hemmings	0
*P.J.L. Dujon	c Smith, b Small	27
E.A. Moseley	c Gooch, b Fraser	0
I.R. Bishop	not out	6
M.D. Marshall		
C.A. Walsh		
	B 12, lb 4, w1, nb 1	18
	TOTAL for 7 wickets (50 overs)	216

	O	M	R	W
Small	9	–	37	2
DeFreitas	10	2	29	1
Capel	9	1	47	–
Fraser	10	–	41	1
Hemmings	10	–	31	3
Gooch	2	–	15	–

Fall of wickets
1–11, 2–23, 3–74, 4–158, 5–158, 6–204, 7–210
Umpires – L.H. Barker & S. Bucknor
Man-of-the-Match – R.B. Richardson

West Indies won by 3 wickets

Fourth One-Day International
WEST INDIES V ENGLAND
at Bourda, Georgetown, Guyana
7 March, 1990

England

G.A. Gooch (capt)	b Moseley	33
W. Larkins	c Richards, b Moseley	34
R.A. Smith	c Hooper, b Walsh	18
A.J. Lamb	c Dujon, b Bishop	21
A.J. Stewart	c Dujon, b Walsh	0
D.J. Capel	b Hooper	1
*R.C. Russell	b Bishop	28
P.A.J. DeFreitas	run out	11
G.C. Small	not out	18
E.E. Hemmings	not out	0
A.R.C. Fraser		
	B 1, lb 9, w 7, nb 7	24
	TOTAL for 8 wickets (48 overs)	188

	O	M	R	W
Bishop	10	1	41	2
Walsh	10	1	33	2
Baptiste	9	3	29	–
Moseley	9	–	44	2
Hooper	10	–	31	1

Fall of wickets
1–71, 2–88, 3–109, 4–109, 5–112, 6–132, 7–156, 8–181

West Indies

D.L. Haynes	c DeFreitas, b Hemmings	50
C.A. Best	run out	100
R.B. Richardson	c Russell, b Capel	19
C.L. Hooper	not out	16
I.V.A. Richards (capt)	c DeFreitas, b Fraser	2
K.L.T. Arthurton	not out	0
*P.J.L. Dujon		
E.A.E. Baptiste		
E.A. Moseley		
I.R. Bishop		
C.A. Walsh		
	lb 2, w 1, nb 1	4
	TOTAL for 4 wickets (45.2 overs)	191

	O	M	R	W
DeFreitas	7	1	32	–
Small	9.2	1	43	–
Capel	9	2	39	1
Fraser	10	1	42	1
Hemmings	10	1	33	1

Fall of wickets
1–113, 2–155, 3–179, 4–182
Umpires – D.M. Archer & C. Duncan
Man-of-the-Match – C.A. Best

West Indies won by 6 wickets

One-Day International
WEST INDIES V ENGLAND
at Bourda, Georgetown, Guyana
15 March, 1990

England

G.A. Gooch (capt)	b Hooper	42
W. Larkins	c and b Bishop	1
R.A. Smith	c Dujon, b Bishop	1
A.J. Lamb	c Best, b Moseley	9
A.J. Stewart	b Hooper	13
R.J. Bailey	c and b Ambrose	42
D.J. Capel	c Dujon, b Ambrose	7
*R.C. Russell	c Best, b Ambrose	19
G.C. Small	c Dujon, b Ambrose	0
E.E. Hemmings	not out	3
A.R.C. Fraser	not out	3
	B 2, lb 9, w 12, nb 3	26
	TOTAL for 9 wickets (49 overs)	166

	O	M	R	W
Bishop	7	2	22	2
Ambrose	9	1	19	4
Moseley	10	1	48	1
Baptiste	10	1	30	–
Hooper	10	–	28	2
Best	3	–	8	–

Fall of wickets
1–13, 2–18, 3–47, 4–86, 5–89, 6–103, 7–150, 8–151, 9–161

West Indies

C.G. Greenidge	lbw, b Fraser		77
C.B. Lambert	b Hemmings		48
R.B. Richardson	c Capel, b Small		7
C.L. Hooper	not out		19
C.A. Best	not out		7
K.L.T. Arthurton			
*P.J.L. Dujon (capt)			
E.A.E. Baptiste			
E.A. Moseley			
C.E.L. Ambrose			
I.R. Bishop			

lb 2, w4, nb 3   9

TOTAL for 3 wickets (40.2 overs)   167

	O	M	R	W
Capel	9	1	41	–
Small	7	–	32	1
Fraser	9.2	1	33	1
Gooch	5	1	22	–
Hemmings	10	1	37	1

Fall of wickets
1–88, 2–105, 3–152
Umpires – D.M. Archer & C. Duncan
Man-of-the-Match – C.G. Greenidge

West Indies won by 7 wickets
This match was played when the Test match was abandoned

PRESIDENT'S XI V ENGLAND XI
at Guaracara Park, Pointe-à-Pierre, Trinidad
17, 18, 19 and 20 March, 1990

England XI	first innings		second innings	
G.A. Gooch (capt)	c Harris, b Haynes	66	c and b Haynes	61
W. Larkins	c Harris, b Patterson	1	lbw, b Haynes	13
A.J. Stewart	c Adams, b Benjamin	6	b Benjamin	15
R.A. Smith	c Morgan, b Haynes	29	not out	99
R.J. Bailey	lbw, b Baptiste	52	b Haynes	7
D.J. Capel	c Harris, b Arthurton	1	(7) lbw, b Benjamin	0
*R.C. Russell	c Harris, b Baptiste	25	(8) c Lambert, b Haynes	16
P.A.J. DeFreitas	not out	10	(9) lbw, b Haynes	15
C.C. Lewis	lbw, b Patterson	21	(10) lbw, b Haynes	6
E.E. Hemmings	b Baptiste	3	(6) lbw, b Benjamin	1
D.E. Malcolm	b Baptiste	8	b Patterson	4
	lb 5, w 5, nb 20	30	B 10, lb 7, w 3, nb 21	41
	TOTAL	252	TOTAL	278

	O	M	R	W	O	M	R	W
Patterson	9	1	45	2	23.5	7	59	1
Benjamin	15	2	34	1	27	7	70	3
Baptiste	33.1	5	91	4	22	6	42	–
Haynes	32	12	57	2	40	11	90	6
Arthurton	5	–	18	1				
Morgan	1	–	2	–				

Fall of wickets
1–12, 2–36, 3–107, 4–136, 5–150, 6–201, 7–206, 8–239, 9–243;
1–38, 2–98, 3–104, 4–131, 5–132, 6–132, 7–166, 8–209, 9–249

President's XI	first innings		second innings	
C.B. Lambert	b Malcolm	12	c Capel, b Malcolm	0
D.S. Morgan	run out	0	c Bailey, b Malcolm	12
K.L.T. Arthurton	c Russell, b Capel	37	b DeFreitas	2
B.C. Lara	b DeFreitas	134	lbw, b DeFreitas	1
A.L. Logie (capt)	c Russell, b Haynes	40	(6) c and b Hemmings	26
J.C. Adams	lbw, b DeFreitas	8	(5) c Russell, b DeFreitas	8
*L.L. Harris	run out	8	lbw, b Malcolm	0
R.C. Haynes	c Russell, b Malcolm	20	b DeFreitas	30
E.A.E. Baptiste	c and b Malcolm	9	lbw, b Capel	19
K.C.G. Benjamin	c Russell, b DeFreitas	2	not out	6
B.P. Patterson	not out	0	lbw, b Hemmings	11
	B 3, lb 5, w 1, nb 15	24	nb 8	8
	TOTAL	294	TOTAL	123

	O	M	R	W	O	M	R	W
Malcolm	19	4	60	3	11	3	29	3
DeFreitas	26.5	1	89	3	13	2	54	4
Lewis	11	2	47	–				
Capel	9	–	42	1	5	3	9	1
Hemmings	18	5	48	1	7.4	2	31	2

Fall of wickets
1–17, 2–21, 3–98, 4–229, 5–245, 6–260, 7–271, 8–286, 9–292, 1–0;
2–3, 3–6, 4–26, 5–26, 6–26, 7–58, 8–106, 9–110
Umpires – Z. Maccum & M. Hosein
Toss – President's XI

England XI won by 113 runs

Third Test Match
WEST INDIES V ENGLAND
at Queen's Park Oval, Port of Spain, Trinidad
23, 24, 25, 27 and 28 March, 1990

West Indies	first innings		second innings	
C.G. Greenidge	c Stewart, b Malcolm	5	1bw, b Fraser	42
D.L. Haynes (capt)	c Lamb, b Small	0	c Lamb, b Malcolm	45
R.B. Richardson	c Russell, b Fraser	8	c Gooch, b Small	34
C.A. Best	c Lamb, b Fraser	10	lbw, b Malcolm	0
*P.J.L. Dujon	lbw, b Small	4	b Malcolm	0
A.L. Logie	c Lamb, b Fraser	98	c Larkins, b Malcolm	20
C.L. Hooper	c Russell, b Capel	32	run out	10
E.A. Moseley	c Russell, b Malcolm	0	c Lamb, b Malcolm	26
C.E.L. Ambrose	c Russell, b Malcolm	7	c Russell, b Fraser	18
I.R. Bishop	b Malcolm	16	not out	15
C.A. Walsh	not out	8	lbw, b Malcolm	1
	Lb 4, nb 7	11	B 2, lb 13, w 1, nb 12	28
	TOTAL	199	TOTAL	239

	O	M	R	W	O	M	R	W
Small	17	4	41	2	21	8	56	1
Malcolm	20	2	60	4	26.2	5	77	6
Fraser	13.1	2	41	3	24	4	61	2
Capel	15	2	53	1	13	3	30	–

Fall of wickets
1–5, 2–5, 3–22, 4–27, 5–29, 6–92, 7–93, 8–103, 9–177;
1–96, 2–100, 3–100, 4–100, 5–142, 6–167, 7–200, 8–200, 9–234

England	first innings		second innings	
G.A. Gooch (capt)	c Dujon, b Bishop	84	retired hurt	18
W. Larkins	c Dujon, b Ambrose	54	c Dujon, b Moseley	7
A.J. Stewart	c Dujon, b Ambrose	9	c Bishop, b Walsh	31
A.J. Lamb	b Bishop	32	lbw, b Bishop	25
R.A. Smith	c Dujon, b Moseley	5	lbw, b Walsh	2
R.J. Bailey	c Logie, b Moseley	0	b Walsh	0
D.J. Capel	c Moseley, b Ambrose	40	not out	17
*R.C. Russell	c Best, b Walsh	15	not out	5
G.C. Small	lbw, b Bishop	0		
A.R.C. Fraser	c Hooper, b Ambrose	11		
D.E. Malcolm	not out	0		
	B 10, lb 9, w 3, nb 16	38	B 2, 1b 7, nb 6	15

TOTAL 288   TOTAL for 5 wickets 120

	O	M	R	W	O	M	R	W
Bishop	31	6	69	3	10	1	31	1
Ambrose	36.2	8	59	4	6	–	20	–
Walsh	22	5	45	1	7	–	27	3
Hooper	18	5	26	–				
Moseley	30	5	70	2	10	2	33	1

Fall of wickets
1–112, 2–152, 3–195, 4–214, 5–214, 6–214, 7–243, 8–244, 9–284;
1–27, 2–74, 3–79, 4–85, 5–106
Umpires – C.E. Cumberbatch & L.H. Baker
Toss – England

Match Drawn

151

ENGLAND XI V BARBARDOS

at Kensington Oval, Bridgetown, Barbados
30, 31 March and 1 April, 1990

Barbados	first innings		second innings	
C.G. Greenidge	c and b Medlycott	183	c Stewart, b Medlycott	51
D.L. Haynes (capt)	c Bailey, b DeFreitas	9	lbw, b DeFreitas	13
C.A. Best	c DeFreitas, b Medlycott	95	b Lewis	71
T.R.O. Payne	b Medlycott	0	(6) lbw, b Medlycott	13
R.I.C. Holder	lbw, b Hemmings	18	not cut	26
M.D. Marshall	c Lewis, b Hemmings	24	(4) c sub (Bairstow),	
			b Lewis	31
*R. Hoyte	b Hemmings	2		
H. Springer	lbw, b Hemmings	2		
A.L. Johnson	c Lamb, b Hemmings	0		
S. Skeete	c Capel, b Medlycott	1		
V. Walcott	not out	1		
	B 3, lb 8, nb 21	32	B 1, lb 6, nb 9	16
	TOTAL	367	TOTAL for 5 wks., dec.	221

	O	M	R	W	O	M	R	W
DeFreitas	17	1	60	1	13	2	38	1
Lewis	11	1	51	–	13	3	30	2
Capel	10	–	53	–	13	1	50	–
Hemmings	32	12	77	5				
Medlycott	30	3	115	4	33	5	100	2

Fall of wickets
1–32, 2–247, 3–250, 4–289, 5–345, 6–359, 7–365, 8–365, 9–365;
1–24, 2–114, 3–177, 4–186, 5–200

England XI	first innings		second innings	
A.J. Stewart	c Best, b Marshall	21	hit wkt, b Walcott	27
D.J. Capel	c Greenidge, b Marshall	3	not out	51
*R.J. Bailey	c sub, b Walcott	7	not out	27
N. Hussain	not out	70		
R.A. Smith	lbw, b Marshall	1		
D.I. Gower	c Holder, b Johnson	4		
A.J. Lamb (capt)	lbw, b Springer	8		
P.A.J. DeFreitas	lbw, b Springer	10		
C.C. Lewis	c Best, b Walcott	6		
K.T. Medlycott	c Best, b Springer	0		
E.E. Hemmings	b Walcott	0		
	B 8, lb 5, w 2, nb 13	28	B 8, lb 6, w 2, nb 5	21
	TOTAL	158	TOTAL for one wicket	126

	O	M	R	W	O	M	R	W
Marshall	16	3	57	3	5	–	16	–
Skeete	6	1	21	–				
Walcott	12.5	4	25	3	11	1	30	1
Johnson	6	–	21	1	5	2	15	–
Springer	8	1	21	3	12	3	30	–
Best					6	–	15	–
Haynes					3	1	6	–

Fall of wickets
1–25, 2–36, 3–52, 4–56, 5–87, 6–110, 7–128, 8–156, 9–157;
1–49

Umpires – N.D.B. Harrison & S. Parris
Toss – England

Match Drawn

Fifth One-Day International
WEST INDIES V ENGLAND
at Kensington Oval, Bridgetown, Barbados
3 April, 1990

England

D.M. Smith	b Moseley	5
W. Larkins	b Walsh	34
R.A. Smith	run out	69
A.J. Lamb (capt)	not out	55
N. Hussain	not out	15
D.J. Capel		
*R.C. Russell		
P.A.J. DeFreitas		
C.C. Lewis		
G.C. Small		
E.E. Hemmings		
	B 2, lb 8, w 14, nb 12	36
	TOTAL for 3 wickets (38 overs)	214

	O	M	R	W
Ambrose	9	2	31	–
Walsh	8	–	49	1
Moseley	7	–	43	1
Marshall	8	–	50	–
Hooper	6	–	31	–

Fall of wickets
1–47, 2–98, 3–161

West Indies

C.G. Greenidge	c Russell, b Small	6
D.L. Haynes (capt)	c Hussain, b Hemmings	45
R.B. Richardson	b Small	80
C.A. Best	c sub (Stewart), b Capel	51
A.L. Logie	c Larkins, b DeFreitas	2
C.L. Hooper	c Larkins, b Small	12
*P.J.L. Dujon	not out	11
E.A. Moseley	not out	1
M.D. Marshall		
C.A. Walsh		
C.E.L. Ambrose		
	lb 6, w 1, nb 2	9
	TOTAL for 6 wickets (37.3 overs)	217

	O	M	R	W
Small	9	1	29	3
DeFreitas	8.3	-	63	1
Lewis	5	-	35	-
Capel	6	-	53	1
Hemmings	9	-	31	1

Fall of wickets
1–39, 2–78, 3–189, 4–193, 5–199, 6–212

Umpires – L.H. Barker & D.M. Archer
Man-of-the-Match – R.B. Richardson

West Indies won by 4 wickets

Fourth Test Match
WEST INDIES V ENGLAND
at Kensington Oval, Bridgetown, Barbados
5, 6, 7, 8 and 10 April, 1990

West Indies	first innings		second innings	
C.G. Greenidge	c Russell, b DeFreitas	41	lbw, b Small	3
D.L. Haynes	c Stewart, b Small	0	c Malcolm, b Small	109
R.B. Richardson	c Russell, b Small	45	lbw, b DeFreitas	39
C.A. Best	c Russell, b Small	164		
I.V.A. Richards (capt)	c Russell, b Capel	70	(4) c Small, b Capel	12
A.L. Logie	c Russell, b Capel	31	(5) lbw, b DeFreitas	48
*P.J.L. Dujon	b Capel	31	(8) not out	15
M.D. Marshall	c Lamb, b Small	4	(7) c Smith, b Small	7
C.E.L. Ambrose	not out	20	c Capel, b DeFreitas	1
I.R. Bishop	run out	10	not out	11
E.A. Moseley	b DeFreitas	4	(6) b Small	5
	lb 8, nb 18	26	lb 12, w 1, nb 4	17
	TOTAL	446	TOTAL for 8 wkts., dec.	267

	O	M	R	W	O	M	R	W
Malcolm	33	6	142	–	10	–	46	–
Small	35	5	109	4	20	1	74	4
DeFreitas	29.5	5	99	2	22	2	69	3
Capel	24	5	88	3	16	1	66	1

Fall of wickets
1–6, 2–69, 3–108, 4–227, 5–291, 6–395, 7–406, 8–411, 9–431;
1–13, 2–80, 3–109, 4–223, 5–228, 6–238, 7–239

England	first innings		second innings	
A.J Stewart	c Richards, b Moseley	45	c Richards, b Ambrose	37
W. Larkins	c Richardson, b Bishop	0	c Dujon, b Bishop	0
R.J. Bailey	b Bishop	17	c Dujon, b Ambrose	6
A.J. Lamb (capt)	lbw, b Ambrose	119	(6) c Dujon, b Moseley	10
R.A. Smith	b Moseley	62	(7) not out	40
N. Hussain	lbw, b Marshall	18	(8) lbw, b Ambrose	0
D.J. Capel	c Greenidge, b Marshall	2	(9) lbw, b Ambrose	6
*R.C. Russell	lbw, b Bishop	7	(5) b Ambrose	55
P.A.J. DeFreitas	c and b Ambrose	24	(10) lbw, b Ambrose	0
G.C. Small	not out	1	(4) lbw, b Ambrose	0
D.E. Malcolm	b Bishop	12	lbw, b Ambrose	4
	B 14, lb 9, w 3, nb 25	51	B 8, lb 9, w 1, nb 15	33
	TOTAL	358	TOTAL	191

	O	M	R	W	O	M	R	W
Bishop	24.3	8	70	4	20	7	40	1
Ambrose	25	2	82	2	22.4	10	45	8
Moseley	28	2	114	2	19	3	44	1
Marshall	23	6	55	2	18	8	31	–
Richards	9	4	14	–	10	5	11	–
Richardson					2	1	3	–

Fall of wickets
1–1, 2–46, 3–75, 4–268, 5–297, 6–301, 7–308, 8–340, 9–358;
1–1, 2–10, 3–10, 4–71, 5–97, 6–166, 7–173, 8–181, 9–181

Umpires – L.H. Barker & D.M. Archer
Toss – England

West Indies won by 164 runs

Fifth Test Match
WEST INDIES V ENGLAND
at Recreation Ground, St John's, Antigua
12, 14, 15 and 16 April, 1990

England	first innings		second innings	
A.J. Stewart	c Richards, b Walsh	27	c Richardson, b Bishop	8
W. Larkins	c Hooper, b Ambrose	30	b Ambrose	10
R.J. Bailey	c Dujon, b Bishop	42	(4) c Dujon, b Bishop	8
A.J. Lamb (capt)	c Richards, b Ambrose	37	(5) b Baptiste	35
R.A. Smith	lbw, b Walsh	12	(6) retired hurt	8
N. Hussain	c Dujon, b Bishop	35	(7) c Dujon, b Bishop	34
D.J. Capel	c Haynes, b Bishop	10	(8) run out	1
*R.C. Russell	c Dujon, b Bishop	7	(9) c Richardson, b Ambrose	24
P.A.J. DeFreitas	lbw, b Bishop	21	(10) c Greenidge, b Ambrose	0
G.C. Small	lbw, b Walsh	8	(3) b Ambrose	4
D.E. Malcolm	not out	0	not out	1
	B 5, lb 11, nb 15	31	B 1, lb 8, w 1, nb 11	21
	TOTAL	260	TOTAL	154

	O	M	R	W	O	M	R	W
Bishop	28.1	6	84	5	14	2	36	3
Ambrose	29	5	79	2	13	7	22	4
Walsh	21	4	51	3	10	1	40	–
Baptiste	13	4	30	–	10	1	47	1

Fall of wickets
1–42, 2–101, 3–143, 4–167, 5–167, 6–195, 7–212, 8–242, 9–259;
1–16, 2–20, 3–33, 4–37, 5–86, 6–96, 7–148,
8–148, 9–154

158

West Indies	first innings	
C.G. Greenidge	run out	149
D.L. Haynes	c Russell, b Small	167
R.B. Richardson	c Russell, b Malcolm	34
C.L. Hooper	b Capel	1
I.V.A. Richards (capt)	c Smith, b Malcolm	1
A.L. Logie	c Lamb, b DeFreitas	15
*P.J.L. Dujon	run out	25
E.A.E. Baptiste	c Russell, b Malcolm	9
C.E.L. Ambrose	c DeFreitas, b Capel	5
I.R. Bishop	not out	14
C.A. Walsh	b Malcolm	8
	lb 5, nb 13	18
	TOTAL	446

	O	M	R	W
Small	31	3	123	1
Malcolm	34.5	5	126	4
Capel	28	1	118	2
DeFreitas	27	4	74	1

Fall of wickets
1–298, 2–357, 3–358, 4–359, 5–382, 6–384, 7–415, 8–417, 9–433

Umpires – D.M. Archer & A.E. Weekes
Toss – England

West Indies won by an innings and 32 runs

Averages and Statistics

Cable & Wireless Test Series
WEST INDIES V ENGLAND

Averages
West Indies

Batting	M.	Inns	NOs	Runs	H.S.	Average	100s	50s
D.L. Haynes	4	7		371	167	53.00	2	
C.A. Best	3	5		242	164	48.40	1	1
C.G. Greenidge	4	7		308	149	44.00	1	
A.L. Logie	3	5		212	98	42.40		1
I.V.A. Richards	3	5		141	70	28.20		1
R.B. Richardson	4	7		195	45	27.85		
P.J.L. Dujon	4	7	2	109	31	21.80		
I.R. Bishop	4	7	3	69	16	17.25		
C.L. Hooper	3	5		71	32	14.20		
C.E.L. Ambrose	3	5	1	51	20*	12.75		
E.A. Moseley	2	4		35	26	8.75		
M.D. Marshall	2	4	1	19	8	6.33		
C.A. Walsh	3	5	1	25	8	6.25		

Played in one Test – B.P. Patterson 0 & 2
E.A.E. Baptiste 9

Bowling	Overs	Mds	Runs	Wks	Average	Best	10/m	5/in
C.E.L. Ambrose	132	32	307	20	15.35	8/45	1	1
I.R. Bishop	160.1	37	419	21	19.95	5/84		1
C.A. Walsh	93.2	14	243	12	20.25	5/68		1
E.A. Moseley	87	12	261	6	43.50	2/70		
M.D. Marshall	59	17	132	3	44.00	2/55		
E.A.E. Baptiste	23	5	77	1	77.00	1/47		
B.P. Patterson	21	3	85	1	85.00	1/74		
I.V.A. Richards	28	10	47	–	–			
C.L. Hooper	27	6	54	–	–			

Bowled in one innings: C.A. Best 4–0–19–0
R.B. Richardson 2–1–3–0

Fielding Figures
15 – P.J.L. Dujon
　4 – I.V.A. Richards and R.B. Richardson
　3 – C.G. Greenidge, C.A. Best and C.L. Hooper
　1 – D.L. Haynes, I.R. Bishop, B.P. Patterson, A.L. Logie,
　　　E.A. Moseley and C.E.L. Ambrose

England

Batting	M.	Inns	NOs	Runs	H.S.	Average	100s	50s
A.J. Lamb	4	7		390	132	55.71	2	
G.A. Gooch	2	4	1	128	84	42.66		1
R.A. Smith	4	7	2	186	62	37.20		2
W. Larkins	4	8	1	176	54	25.14		1
A.J. Stewart	4	8	1	170	45	24.28		
R.C. Russell	4	7	1	139	55	23.16		1
N. Hussain	3	5		100	35	20.00		
D.J. Capel	4	7	1	81	40	13.50		
A.R.C. Fraser	2	2	1	13	11	13.00		
R.J. Bailey	3	6		73	42	12.16		
P.A.J. DeFreitas	2	4		45	24	11.25		
D.E. Malcolm	4	6	3	17	12	5.66		
G.C. Small	4	6	1	17	8	3.40		

Bowling	Overs	Mds	Runs	Wks	Average	Best	10/m	5/inn
A.R.C. Fraser	71.1	19	161	11	14.63	5/28		1
G.C. Small	161	33	505	17	29.70	4/58		
D.E. Malcolm	161.4	24	577	19	30.36	6/77	1	1
P.A.J. DeFreitas	78.5	11	242	6	40.33	3/69		
D.J.Capel	124	17	436	9	48.44	3/88		

Fielding Figures
14 – R.C. Russell
 7 – A.J. Lamb
 4 – W. Larkins
 3 – G.C. Small
 2 – G.A. Gooch, A.J. Stewart, R.A. Smith and D.J. Capel
 1 – N. Hussain, D.E. Malcolm and P.A.J. DeFreitas

England in the West Indies

First-Class Matches
P. 9, won 2, drawn 4, lost 3
Test Matches
P. 4, won 1, drawn 1, lost 2
One-Day Internationals
P. 6, lost 4, abandoned 2
All Matches
P. 16, won 3, drawn 6, lost 7

First Class Averages –

Batting	M.	Inns	NOs	Runs	H.S.	Average	100s	50s
G.A. Gooch	6	11	1	616	239	61.60	1	4
A.J. Lamb	7	12		549	132	45.75	2	1
W. Larkins	8	16	2	542	124*	37.42	2	1
R.A. Smith	9	16	3	477	99*	36.69		4
A.J. Stewart	9	18	1	516	125	30.35	1	1
N. Hussain	6	10	1	260	70*	28.88		1
R.C. Russell	8	15	5	269	55	26.90		1
D.J. Capel	8	15	3	245	65	20.41		2
R.J. Bailey	6	12	1	177	52	16.09		1
P.A.J. DeFreitas	6	11	4	108	24	15.42		
C.C. Lewis	2	3		33	21	11.00		
K.T. Medlycott	3	3		24	21	8.00		
D.E. Malcolm	7	9	3	29	12	4.83		
A.R.C. Fraser	4	5	1	17	11	4.25		
G.C. Small	5	6	1	17	8	3.40		
E.E. Hemmings	4	6	1	13	6	2.60		

Played in one match –   D.I. Gower 4

Centuries

A.J. Lamb (2)	132 v West Indies, Kingston, First Test
	119 v West Indies, Bridgetown, Fourth Test
W. Larkins (2)	124 not out v Jamaica, Kingston
	107 v Leeward Islands, Basseterre
G.A. Gooch (1)	239 v Jamaica, Kingston
A.J. Stewart (1)	125 v Leeward Islands, Basseterre

Century Partnerships
First Wicket
145 G.A. Gooch and W. Larkins v Jamaica, Kingston (first innings)
137 A.J. Stewart and W. Larkins v Jamaica, Kingston (second innings)
112 G.A. Gooch and W. Larkins, Third Test Match, Port of Spain

Second Wicket
124 W. Larkins and A.J. Stewart v Leeward Islands, Basseterre

Third Wicket
144 A.J. Stewart and R.A. Smith v Leeward Islands, Basseterre
152 A.J. Stewart and A.J. Lamb v Windward Islands, Castries

Fourth Wicket
172 A.J. Lamb and R.A. Smith, First Test, Kingston
193 A.J. Lamb and R.A. Smith, Fourth Test, Bridgetown

Bowling	Overs	Mds	Runs	Wks	Average	Best	10/m	5/inn
E.E. Hemmings	108.1	30	301	15	20.06	5/77		1
A.R.C. Fraser	122.2	27	353	17	20.76	5/28		1
G.C. Small	201	40	644	23	28.00	4/58		
D.E. Malcolm	258.4	40	948	32	29.62	6/77	1	1
K.T. Medlycott	110.2	12	425	13	32.69	4/36		
P.A.J. DeFreitas	196.4	26	697	21	33.19	4/54		
D.J. Capel	201	26	733	14	52.35	3/88		
C.C. Lewis	35	6	128	2	64.00	2/30		
Bowled in one innings –		G.A. Gooch 3–0–6–1						

Five Wickets in an Innings
E.E. Hemmings (1)   5 for 77 v Barbados, Bridgetown
A.R.C. Fraser (1)   5 for 28, First Test Match, Kingston
D.E. Malcolm (1)   6 for 77, Third Test Match, Port of Spain
(Malcolm took 10 for 137 in this match)

Fielding Figures

26 – R.C. Russell (ct 24/st 2)

 9 – A.J. Lamb

 6 – G.A. Gooch

 5 – R.A. Smith and D.J. Capel

 4 – G.C. Small, A.J. Stewart and W. Larkins

 3 – D.E. Malcolm and R.J. Bailey

 2 – N. Hussain, A.R.C. Fraser, E.E. Hemmings and
    P.A.J. DeFreitas

 1 – K.T. Medlycott, C.C. Lewis and sub (D.L. Bairstow)

List of Players

Graham Gooch

Allan Lamb
Robert Bailey
David Capel
Phillip DeFreitas
Ricky Ellcock
Angus Fraser
David Gower
Eddie Hemmings
Nasser Hussain
Wayne Larkins
Chris Lewis
Devon Malcolm
Keith Medlycott
Jack Russell
Gladstone Small
David Smith
Robin Smith
Alec Stewart

Officials:
Peter Lush
Micky Stewart
Laurie Brown
Peter Austin

ALLAN LAMB (Joe), Northants

Born Langebaanweg, Cape Province, South Africa,
20 June 54

Not only was Allan Lamb my vice-captain, he and I are
almost the same age and we think along the same lines
about cricket, so it was to be expected that he was the
one I discussed most things with on this tour.

He is an exceptional player. I have no hesitation in
saying that on present form he is one of the best batsmen
in the world. He is a real little fighter and he liked
nothing more than to take on the West Indies bowlers
and show them who was the boss. He was a very fine
all-round fielder for many years, but his recent shoulder
operation has confined him to the ring or in the slips or
gully.

His two centuries in the series were magnificent and
reminded everyone what a great player he is. But once it
was all over for the day, there was another side to him
– a restless, energetic person who couldn't sit still for
a minute. If there was anything to be organized, like a
fishing trip or a boat ride, you could bet Lambie would
be organizing it.

I used to call him Joe (his middle name is Joseph) –
and it seemed to sum him up nicely.

ROB BAILEY (Russ), Northants
Born Biddulph, Staffs, 28 October 63

It was a tough tour for Rob, but he took all his disappointments well – even the suspect decision he got at a critical point in the Barbados Test. Cricket can be a tough taskmaster, as Rob certainly found out; but he was always cheerful and always ready with a joke – in fact, a model tourist.

We worked him as hard as anyone in the nets in an effort to adapt his technique to West Indies conditions, but we already knew he was a good player after the one Test he played in 1988. Though he usually fields at slip for his county, Rob proved himself a sound fielder in most positions on tour.

Rob was known to everyone as Russ because of his likeness to the comedian Russ Abbot, and I even found myself introducing him as Russ Bailey to local dignitaries at official occasions.

DAVID CAPEL (Capes), Northants

Born Northampton, 6 February 63

Capes, as he was known to everyone, was one of the keenest, most dedicated players in the party – so much so that he was really down and despondent if things didn't go well for him.

He can bowl the occasional very quick ball, though generally he was about a yard slower than Small or Fraser. If he can add a bit more venom to his bowling and maintain the standard of his batting, which really served us well in Trinidad, he could clinch the England all-rounder's spot for some time to come. A good fielder, he generally played at gully in the Tests.

PHIL DEFREITAS (Daffy), Lancashire.

Born Dominica, 18 February 66

Daffy has been around the Test scene for three or four years now without making a place his own. But on this tour he showed a lot more maturity, was always ready to join in the fun, and when Gus Fraser was injured he bowled very well in his place.

He is another player who could fill the all-rounder's spot. He has plenty of talent, but I would like to see just a little more fire in his bowling. I also hope that Lancashire gives Daffy the chance to move up the order so that he can develop into a serious batsman. He worked hard on this trip and it was starting to pay off for him. He is a superb outfielder – very quick, with safe hands and a very good arm.

RICKY ELLCOCK (Ricky), Middlesex

Born Barbados, 17 June 65

I never really got to know Ricky as he wasn't with us long before he had to return home with back trouble. After we had come back, I saw him at Lord's when Essex played Middlesex in the first match of the season. He had had the operation on his back and would be out of the game for the whole of the 1990 season. But other fast bowlers, notably Neil Foster, have come back from similar operations with their talent unimpaired, and I fully expect Ricky to do the same. He was desperately upset when he had to give up the tour, but I knew he would be sensible enough not to rush things and make sure he was fully fit before he played again.

ANGUS FRASER (Gussie), Middlesex

Born Billinge, Lancashire, 8 August 65

We really missed Gussie when he couldn't play in the last couple of Tests, and I know he was bitterly disappointed too. I'm not saying the West Indies were frightened of him, but they had really come to respect him.

In his quiet, droll way, Gus was quite a character to have around on tour. He always had a word or a remark for any situation, which isn't surprising in somebody brought up in the Middlesex atmosphere, with chirpy characters like John Emburey and Mike Gatting to contend with.

DAVID GOWER (Lulu), Hampshire

Born Tunbridge Wells, 1 April 57.

I'll always be grateful to David for putting himself at England's disposal in Barbados and Antigua when we were in trouble with injuries. He was on a hiding to nothing: he had hardly held a bat for six months and he could have easily said he didn't feel he was in a position to help.

But David is an England man through and through, and he would never let us down. I just hope he makes a stack of runs for his new county and comes back into the Test side, which is where he belongs. His record speaks for itself. In the field he is superlative in the covers (though his throw, like Allan Lamb's, is 'gone' after a shoulder operation) and is also good in the slips.

EDDIE HEMMINGS (Spermo), Notts
Born Leamington, 20 February 49

Eddie's generous proportions first of all earned him the nickname of 'whales', which we somehow managed to change to Spermo, in memory of the sperm whale. But don't think the little extra weight that Eddie carried in front made him any less useful.

He has been around for nearly 25 years with Warwickshire and Notts, but he was still as keen as ever on tour in the West Indies, trying like mad in the field (usually at mid-on or mid-off) and always ready to pass on any of the vast store of cricket knowhow he has picked up.

Eddie was selected as our first spinner, but he knew – and readily accepted – the likelihood that he would not be needed for the Tests. A great tourist, he was never heard to complain about not being picked for the big ones, and he made useful contributions in several of the other matches.

NASSER HUSSAIN (Nashwan), Essex
Born Madras, India, 28 March 68

Nasser learned a great deal about Test cricket while he was in the West Indies and I'm confident he will turn it to good use. As I wrote this he was still recovering from the broken wrist he received in Guyana which undoubtedly affected his play in the subsequent matches before the fracture was identified.

We called him Nashwan, which sounds a bit like Nasser, after the horse that won the Derby and the Two Thousand Guineas in 1989. As a batsman he certainly shows indications of being a thoroughbred. His very fast reactions make him an excellent close fielder; in the West Indies we used him mainly in the bad-pad position.

WAYNE LARKINS (Ned), Northants

Born Roxton, Beds, 22 November 53

You've only got to see Ned Larkins in full cry to know he is a batsman of exceptional class. For a long time he was overlooked on account of a rather bad report he received after a tour of Australia in 1979, when he sometimes became bored with not playing. But I was convinced this exclusion had gone on long enough and was delighted when he was selected for this tour. He had, of course, been picked more recently for Tests in England, but had been forced to drop out through injury. Now he is back it is up to him how long he remains.

He was bitterly disappointed at making a pair in the Barbados Test and then by the way he was out in Antigua when they came off for the light only a couple of balls later. But he has been around a long time, he knows a lot about the game, and he is a very useful man to have on your side. He's a good all-round fielder, with safe hands and a fine arm. We used him mainly in the slips.

CHRIS LEWIS (C.C.), Leicestershire

Born Georgetown, Guyana, 14 February 68

I knew very little about C.C. before he joined us when Ricky Ellcock had to go home – but I immediately liked what I saw. He is a lively bowler who can be distinctly sharp, he is a brilliant fielder in almost any position (he plays at slip for his county, but was in the outfield on tour), and could develop into a handy batsman: another serious contender for the all-rounder's place.

Why the nickname C.C? Well, with Christian names of Christopher Clairmonte, what else could we call him?

DEVON MALCOLM (Dev), Derbyshire

Born Kingston, Jamaica, 22 February 63

Dev was one of the successes of the tour and I can see no reason why he should not be part of the England scene for a good many years to come. He was inexperienced and raw, but he knew that and he worked hard on the things we were teaching him. He has a superb physique and he is very quick – make no mistake about that.

He is a quiet lad and was very popular with the rest of the team. He used to take his fair share of leg pulling about his eyesight (he wears 'contacts' when playing, 'specs' when not) – but he could dish it out as well.

KEITH MEDLYCOTT (Medders), Surrey.

Born Whitechapel, London, 12 May 65

I knew before we reached the West Indies that Medders was not going to get much cricket out there. He was taken as cover for Eddie Hemmings, and it was obvious the West Indies were not going to produce wickets to help spinners.

But he gained a lot of useful experience, which was one of the reasons for taking him, and his attitude was always cheerful and helpful. It was useful to have him in case Eddie was ever injured.

There is room for improvement in his bowling, but he knows that and is prepared to work at it. He is a big spinner of the ball and if he works hard he will be in contention to play for England for a number of years yet.

He is a useful batsman and he fields well (he's regularly at slip for his county). At just 25 he is still young for a spinner and has time on his side.

JACK RUSSELL (Jack) Gloucestershire.

Born Stroud, 15 August 63

There's not much more I can say about Jack. He has come on in leaps and bounds, and if I had to pick a current world XI he would unquestionably be the wicket keeper – at present he's the very best around. What's more, his batting has progressed to the point where he can now claim to be a genuine all-rounder. Not yet, perhaps, so great a keeper as Bob Taylor nor so prolific a batsman as Alan Knott, he seems set fair to equal the achievements of those illustrious predecessors in the England side. Add to his technical gifts a really fierce competitive edge, and you know he's one of those players you want around you in a crisis.

Jack has reached where he is by hard work: he is the model of a dedicated professional.

GLADSTONE SMALL (Stony), Warwickshire
Born Barbados, 18 October 61

Like Gus Fraser, he was one of the mainstays of our bowling. He's 28 now and has had his share of injury problems, but he came good in the final Test against Australia in the summer of 1989 and has become an excellent international bowler.

His control is first class, he gives very little away, and if he can start the ball moving away regularly from the batsman, which he must do in England, he will be immensely successful.

On tour he was a credit to the team: he never complained, always got on with the job, would do anything you asked, and was always very popular.

DAVID SMITH (Smudge), Sussex

Born Balham, London, 9 January 56

Smudge was just unlucky: he answered our call when I broke my finger, he was keen, his attitude was just right – and then he broke his thumb in the first match he played.

It's not necessarily the end of the Test road for him. It's true he was taken out to the West Indies on a horses-for-courses basis – he is a good and fearless player of fast bowling – but anyone who scores enough runs in county cricket will always be in contention.

ROBIN SMITH (Judge), Hampshire

Born Durban, South Africa, 13 September 63

A genuinely nice guy who never has a bad word to say about anybody, Judge (because his hair looks like a wig) was nothing but good news on this tour. He came in for a fair amount of ribbing, but he and Allan Lamb were the two rock-solid players in our middle order.

Judge has the same fighting spirit as Lamb, probably born of their South African background. He loves taking on the fast bowlers. But he was always prepared to knuckle down for the sake of the team – a quality that was never better demonstrated than during his long innings for little more than 30 when we were fighting to save the Test in Barbados. A good all-round fielder, he played mainly at slip or gully in the West Indies.

ALEC STEWART (Stewie), Surrey

Born Merton, 8 April 63

Stewie is an interesting character. He's definitely a chip off the old block – chirpy and confident like his father. He has a lot of talent and I think he'll be around on the England scene for a long time.

He found out what Test cricket is all about on this tour, having to go in first after I was injured – and opening against the West Indies in their own backyard is the toughest job in cricket.

He made some useful scores in the 30s and 40s, but he was bitterly disappointed not to go on and make a big one.

He likes to go for his shots, and I wouldn't try to curb him. All he has to do is to determine which shots are getting him out and then to cut them out of his game. I hope he sticks to his wicket-keeping with Surrey; it will give him two strings to his bow, and will be very handy when England are on tour. When not behind the stumps, Stewie is good at slip or short leg – though his good arm makes him useful in the outfield too.